RHETORIC OF REVOLT

RHETORIC OF REVOLT

HO CHI MINH'S DISCOURSE
FOR REVOLUTION

Peter A. DeCaro

Westport, Connecticut
London

Library of Congress Cataloging-in-Publication Data

DeCaro, Peter Anthony.
    Rhetoric of revolt : Ho Chi Minh's discourse for revolution / Peter A. DeCaro.
    p. cm.
    Includes bibliographical references and index.
    ISBN 0-275-97411-1 (alk. paper)
    1. Há, Châ Minh, 1890–1969—Views on revolutions. 2. Há, Châ Minh,
    1890–1969—Language. 3. Vietnam—History—20th century. I. Title.
DS560.72.H6 D3813 2003
959.704'092—dc21   2002025304

British Library Cataloguing in Publication Data is available.

Library of Congress Catalog Card Number: 2002025304
ISBN: 0-275-97411-1

First published in 2003

Praeger Publishers, 88 Post Road West, Westport, CT 06881
An imprint of Greenwood Publishing Group, Inc.
www.praeger.com

Printed in the United States of America

∞™

The paper used in this book complies with the
Permanent Paper Standard issued by the National
Information Standards Organization (Z39.48-1984).

10 9 8 7 6 5 4 3 2 1

Contents

1

Introduction

"The French imperialists' inhuman oppression and exploitation have helped our people realize that with revolution we will survive and without revolution we will die."[1]

—Ho Chi Minh

The imposition of French rule on the country of Vietnam in the latter half of the nineteenth century brought in its wake greater changes than any that had taken place during the preceding two thousand years.[2] France severed Vietnam into three parts—Tonkin, Annam, and Cochin China—and merged them into a French-run colonial territory known as Indochina, which included Cambodia and Laos.[3] Colonial conquest deprived the Vietnamese of the right to call their country by its proper name and think of themselves as Vietnamese.[4] Despite memories of national unity conjured up by the name Vietnam, the division of the country under colonial rule was a real and painful one.[5] Cities, roads, railways, bridges, and ports were built,[6] transforming the economic life of Vietnam from a "family consumption and bartering system" to a "monetary system of cash" for family needs and taxes. However, the new monetary sector of the economy was neither large enough nor sufficient enough to permit extensive peasant employment for wages or a market for agricultural surplus at stable prices.[7] This led to a deterioration of social cohesion.

Traditional culture, values, social structure, and government were challenged, destroyed, and replaced.[8] New land was cleared or drained and put into agricultural production, creating an elite class of Vietnamese landowners. At the same time, Western industry was introduced (and with it came a population explosion) and European educational systems were established for, and produced generations of, young elitist Vietnamese who had little in common with their elders.[9]

Welded together by common feelings of discontent, by a burning desire to restore national independence, and with it national self-respect, the Vietnamese generated few ideas about the future. Returning to the old culture was not possible in the twentieth century, but they had nothing positive to offer in its place—other than the negative goal of driving out the French[10]—until the emergence of Ho Chi Minh.[11]

All revolutions have to face the forces of counterrevolution, supported usually by interventionist powers. In Vietnam's case the internal counterrevolutionary forces at the close of World War II were not a particularly powerful threat to the revolutionary government.[12] Despite the claims of Western imperialist apologists, few revolutions in history have owed less to any form of external aid than the revolution in Vietnam.[13] If left to themselves the Vietnamese would have set about the reconstruction of their society, distorted by eighty-seven years of colonial rule, in accordance with the International Communist Party's general theory of national-democratic, followed by socialist, revolution.[14] But the forces of great-power intervention did not permit this kind of peaceful, progressive development.

Critical historical research by the government of the United States into the political and military involvement of Vietnam's Franco–Vietminh war and subsequent civil war has uncovered a number of controversial issues that range from U.S. justification for intervention on behalf of the French government during the 1940s and 1950s to the commanding role the United States assumed during the 1960s and 1970s. Scores of scholars, historians, journalists, and others worldwide have accurately, and not so accurately, illuminated these issues. However, for all but a few, these illuminations have been premised on Western political ideologies and philosophies;[15] few have derived from the Vietnamese perspective, and fewer, still, have attempted to address the rhetorical discourse from the Vietnamese perspective. Discounting official Vietnamese government publications, I have not, to this date, discovered critical rhetorical analysis of Ho Chi Minh,[16] the progenitor of contemporary Vietnam's independent state.[17] As a result, Western rhetorical critics know very little about Vietnamese communication methodologies and practices, and, for that matter, about Far East Asian rhetorical theories in general.[18]

Ho's revolutionary course of action, primarily animated by a passionate desire for the emancipation of Vietnam from French colonialism, established him as one of the extraordinary figures in this era—part Ghandi, part Lenin, all Vietnamese. He was, perhaps more than any single man of the twentieth century, the living embodiment to his own people—and to the world—of their revolution.[19] More than any other cultural force, Ho's rhetorical discourse brought greater unification to Vietnamese society because, in the struggle against France, this modern revolutionary leader had created a common bond with the peasants which enabled him to wage war successfully.[20] He was one of the rare men in history who perfectly understood and reflected the aspirations of his people.[21] To the Vietnamese, he had earned the title of "Uncle Ho"[22] and, by the French and in the West, he was viewed as a "communist agitator."[23]

Considered by many to have been a symbol of Vietnamese thought and character, Ho Chi Minh overcame insurmountable odds and became the driving force behind Vietnam's independence from France in 1945; during the French reoccupation of Vietnam in 1946, until their defeat at Dien Bien Phu in 1954; and again during U.S. intervention beginning with the Eisenhower administration until U.S. defeat in 1974. No other leader of the twentieth century can claim such achievements, or the ability to unite a divided people and sustain a revolution for as many years as Ho did.

Ho Chi Minh and the war in Vietnam is a prima fascia example of how the failure of the United States to understand Vietnamese politics proved to be disastrous. The goal of this text is to illuminate a rhetoric based on non-Aristotelian precepts—chiefly, Vietnamese. More specifically, this text explicates the "reconstitutive rhetoric"[24] of Ho Chi Minh and explains the reasons for its effectiveness. This endeavor is necessary because we, in the West, should make every effort to strive for a better understanding of those who are different than ourselves so calamitous events such as U.S. participation in Vietnamese sovereignty can be avoided.

BACKGROUND

Ho Chi Minh's death on 3 September 1969, at the age of seventy-nine, brought to an end fifty years of active political life and marked the close of a revolutionary era in Vietnamese history. The Vietnamese Communist Party owes its preeminent position in Vietnam today to the strength and stability of its leadership, and no man was more instrumental in providing this leadership than Ho Chi Minh.

Ho left his native land of central Vietnam at the age of twenty-one to travel abroad. He was the leader of the Indochinese Communist Party in the 1930s and returned to Vietnam during World War II to lead the liberation movement against French rule. Ho founded the Vietminh and brought it to victory over the French. Claiming himself President of the Democratic Republic of Vietnam on 2 September 1945, he held this office for twenty-four years, until his death. For his countrymen, he personified their heroic and ceaseless struggle for independence from foreign domination.[25]

While there are numerous biographies detailing Ho's life and struggles, none addresses the combination of his rhetorical persona and discourse as an inextricable central theme that enabled him to reconstitute the collective minds of the Vietnamese as a nation and thus move them to sustain a struggle for independence that lasted thirty years.

Ho Chi Minh's rhetorical prowess for the audiences that comprised the independent movement in French colonial Indochina was clearly the *sine qua non* of his career. That prowess is as puzzling as it is undeniable. Ho's persuasion parallels the lingering inability to understand the nationalist movements and their appeal in Far East Asia in the period between the two world wars. Ho's rhetoric exemplifies how Vietnamese nationalism and cultural heritage invited and can be effectively embodied in the rhetor's substantive themes and arguments, second persona, and first or personal persona. Based on this analysis, I suggest that when these rhetorical components, combined with cultural heritage, are reciprocal and complementary, as in the case of Ho Chi Minh, they comprise a rhetorical formula[26] that helps explain his persuasion. In their most potent form, the rhetorical components seem to coalesce in a merger of the rhetor's thought and character that can reconstitute individuals into audiences capable of carrying out nationalist policies.[27]

If we look at ourselves critically, our principled beliefs, at times, have given rise to cultural chauvinism. They help us to justify our economic tyranny over the Third World, propel us confidently into our "Vietnams," and are our warrant for pronouncing judgment on the cultural standards of other nations.[28] These negative consequences go some way toward subverting our erstwhile ideals. There has been a tendency to exaggerate the Westernization aspect of the human being in the definition of humanity. This prejudice has fostered an unwarranted confidence in the quality of our own cultural achievements and social institutions.[29]

The problem for our tradition has been simple yet enduring: When are we going to consider the linguistic, communicative, and conceptual barriers of other cultures, especially the Sino/Vietnamese cultures?[30] The temptation to construe an alien culture in the more comfortable terms of one's own interpretive constructs is altogether too powerful to ignore. The dogmatism of some analytic philosopher, rhetorician, politician, or government official is no less detrimental to an understanding of Far East Asian philosophy, communication, and culture than was the theological dogmatism of previous generations of translators and interpreters who introduced this region of the world to the West.

There are specific ideological and communicative barriers standing between the Far East and the West. One would certainly want to take seriously the importance of Marxist ideology in China and Vietnam. These countries are opening their doors to other cultures, forms of thinking, communication patterns, and languages in a most dramatic manner. Marxism is no longer the only perspective from which to interpret the Chinese and Vietnamese or from which they view the world. This is but to say that Marxism may be fading as an ideology and may soon exist only in the form of a philosophy, a form in which its principal contentions may be discussed and debated.[31]

The West believes that the ideology undergirding its technological societies is eminently exportable. Inherent in the technological state of mind is the belief that scientific and technological progress is essential to the attainment and maintenance of an acceptable standard of human life on the surface of this planet. We have a true missionary zeal for exporting our ideology to our neighbors. Such zeal is a consequence of our essentially quantitative mode of thinking in economics and science, which leads us to be perhaps overly impressed by our *measurable* successes. And as a result, we have lost sight of our culture's aesthetics.[32]

We are faced with a most interesting dilemma. In order for many Third World countries in the Far East—notably China and Vietnam—to compete in the global economy of the twenty-first century, they have no choice but to import

Western science and technologies.[33] And although it would be an exaggeration to say that the West likewise has no choice but to seek out the intellectual and cultural resources of the Chinese and Vietnamese, failure to do so carries with it great risk.

The United States can no longer compel other countries to accept economic imperialism supported by threats of militarism. There is but one means of effective international cooperation: meaningful dialogue. The increased possibilities for dialogue are partly a result of a transformation of the Western philosophic and communicative scenes, away from the dogmatic forms of thinking and communicating. But this transformation has been too slow in developing, especially in cross-cultural understanding and the communication process. The central problem is that while one may recognize that negotiating internationally is difficult in coping with a wider range of decision-making styles, perception of objectives, or thought processes than would be encountered at home, "cultural factors" is a vague and fuzzy concept not easily translated into practical application.[34] A cross-cultural dimension is recognized, in effect, simply by anticipating that there will probably be something "foreign" when communicating, whether in business, politics, or simply engaging in friendly conversation. When cultural contrasts are more pronounced, potential for misunderstanding will be greater, and more time will be lost in talking past each other. More complete explanations of one's positions, a thorough understanding of the "other's" positions, or a special kind of persuasive skill may be called for.[35]

The cultural difference that has to be taken into account may turn out to be as important as that found in certain contrasting sets of values that determine the hierarchy of negotiating objectives themselves, or as trivial as behavior mannerisms that subtly block confidence and trust. Thus, across the board, these matters require studied attention as one tries to capture the logic and intent of the other side or tries to be persuasive or assure that one's own position is understood without misperception or distortion. For these things to occur, there must exist research that fleshes out cultural properties influencing the communication process.

While breaking ground is almost an impossible task in some specialized areas, this topic offers significant opportunities. Rhetorical scholarship has had little or nothing to offer concerning Ho Chi Minh. This text is, therefore, justified for three basic reasons. First, the basis for examining Ho's form of rhetoric is founded on the dearth of biographical research concerning Ho because of the "impossible" accomplishments realized by him and his rag-tag band of guerrillas. I found only one communication study that examined Ho's discourse from a rhetorical perspective, that is Tran Van Dinh's "The Rhetoric of Revolt: Ho Chi Minh as Communicator." However, I did discover one text by Hue-tam Ho Tai, *Radicalism and the Origins of the Vietnamese Revolution,* that devotes a few passages to Ho's rhetoric.[36] Except for Tran's and Hue-tam's works, no published U.S. communication study focuses on the rhetorical aspects of Ho Chi Minh. This text fills that void by critiquing selected rhetorical extants that were meant to "reconstitute" and "move" his Vietnamese audience.

Second, communication scholars that illuminate the "thought"[37] aspect of reconstitutive rhetorical study do so from a Western ethnocentric position, as a result handicapping their ability to understand fully the rhetorical dynamics of other cultures, especially Far East Asian culture, and specifically Sino/Vietnamese culture. A comprehensive investigation of the Sino/Vietnamese philosophical foundation fills the void created by this ethnocentric approach.

Third, few scholars are familiar with the political and philosophical foundations of the Sino/Vietnamese culture that constitute the "character" of the classical prototypical leader. Illumination of those elements that constitute "character" fill this gap.

NOTES

1. Ho Chi Minh, "Appeal Made by Comrade Nguyen Ai Quoc on the Occasion of the Founding of the Party 3 February 1930," Hanoi Domestic Service in Vietnamese, 0430 GMT, 28 May 1971, located at the Indochina Institute, University of California–Berkeley: File DRV, Subj BIOG, Date February 1930, Subcategory: Ho Chi Minh.

2. Sibnarayan Ray, *Vietnam Seen from East and West* (New York: Frederick A. Praeger, 1966), 22.

3. John T. McAlister Jr. and Paul Mus, *The Vietnamese and Their Revolution* (New York: Harper and Row, 1970), 24.

4. Hue-Tam Ho Tai, *Radicalism and the Origins of the Vietnamese Revolution* (Cambridge: Harvard University Press, 1992), 7.

5. Ibid.

6. Ray, *Vietnam Seen from East and West*, 23.

7. John T. McAlister Jr., *Vietnam: The Origins of Revolution* (New York: Alfred A. Knopf, 1969), 75.

8. Ray, *Vietnam Seen from East and West*, 23.

9. Ibid.

10. Ibid.

11. Ho Chi Minh's former name was Nguyen Ai Quoc ("Nguyen the Patriot"), which he assumed from approximately 1919 until 1942. (There is no general consensus as to the actual name change. Earliest reports put it in 1942, others in 1944.) Ho Chi Minh officially translated means "Ho with the clear will"; however, other translations of the name are current in the West: "Ho, the bringer of light," "Ho, the bright light," "Ho, the enlightener," and "Ho, who has become wise." See Reinhold Neumann-Hoditz, *Portrait of Ho Chi Minh: An Illustrated Biography*, trans. John Hargreaves (Hamburg: Herder and Herder United States, 1972), 135. Ralph Smith states that Nguyen Ai Quoc spent all of 1942 and the first month of 1943 in a Chinese prison. While there, he convinced the Chinese strongman Chang Fakwei of his willingness to join his organization, and was released from prison under the name of Ho Chi Minh. See Ralph Smith, *Viet-Nam and the West* (Ithaca, N.Y.: Cornell University Press, 1971), 110–111. Jean Sainteny writes that Nguyen Ai Quoc assumed the name of Ho Chi Minh—("He Who Enlightens") in order to journey covertly into China as a blind peasant. See Jean Sainteny, *Ho Chi Minh and His Vietnam: A Personal Memoir* (Chicago: Cowles Book Company, 1972), 34–35.

12. Thomas Hodgkin, *Vietnam: The Revolutionary Path* (London: Macmillan, 1981), 334.

13. Ibid.

14. Ibid.

15. See, for example, Robert T. Oliver, "The Rhetorical Tradition in China: Confucius and Mencius," *Today's Speech* 17 (February 1969), 3–8; Beatrice Reynolds, "Lao Tzu: Persuasion through Inaction and Non-Speaking," *Today's Speech* 17 (February 1969), 23–25; James Crump and John Dreher, "Peripatetic Rhetors of the Warring Kingdoms," *Central States Speech Journal* 2 (March 1951), 15–17; and John Dreher and James Crump, "Pre-Han Persuasion: The Legalist School," *Central States Speech Journal* 3 (March 1952), 10–14. This article consists almost entirely of D.K. Liao's translation of Han Feizi's essay, "The Difficulties of Persuasion," from the book that bears his name. For a much superior translation, see Burton Watson, trans., *Han Fei Tzu Basic Writings* (New York: Columbia University Press, 1964), 73–79.

16. This is a rhetorical analysis of Ho Chi Minh; as such, criticism of ruthlessness, political blunders, et cetera are not mentioned. However, he was ruthless in his dealings with anyone he felt posed a threat to his cause, be that friend or foe. As a rule he would have that person assassinated or jailed. Ho did make a number of political miscalculations, especially when dealing with the Chinese prior to 1945, and major calculations when negotiating with the French and the United States during the period 1945–1946. It is not my intent to portray Ho Chi Minh as saintly; he was, in fact, just the opposite.

17. N. Khac Huyen writes, "While a great deal has been said of the Vietnam war, very little has been written about Ho Chi Minh. . . . Ho successfully exploited the impatience of the West and its ignorance of his motives and goals. While Ho's understanding of the West was more than adequate, the West's evaluation of Ho has been tragically defective. Many Western diplomats, politicians, scholars, and, notably, reporters often attributed ideas and policies to Ho, ideas and policies that had not even entered his mind. These assumptions, ironically, often became self-fulfilling prophecies. Ho reacted to the West the way the West saw him, and he usually emerged as the winner." See N. Khac Huyen, *Vision Accomplished? The Enigma of Ho Chi Minh* (New York: Macmillan, 1971), xi–xii.

18. Mary Garrett states that aside from a few brief articles, communication scholars virtually ignored the Chinese rhetorical tradition until Robert Oliver's groundbreaking *Culture and Communication in Ancient India and China* (Syracuse, N.Y.: Syracuse University Press, 1971), in which he provides a comprehensive survey of the classical rhetorics of both cultures. For a more extensive review, see Mary Garrett, "Asian Challenge," reprinted by Sonja K. Foss, Karen A. Foss, and Robert Trapp, eds., *Contemporary Perspectives on Rhetoric* (Prospect Heights, Ill: Waveland, 1991).

19. David Halberstam, *Ho* (New York: Random House, 1971), 12.

20. McAlister, *Vietnam*, 101.

21. William Warby, *Ho Chi Minh and the Struggle for an Independent Vietnam* (London: Merlin, 1972), vi.

22. Halberstam, *Ho*, 12. Also, "Uncle" is a term of endearment usually bestowed on members of the family or very close members of the family. In this context, "Uncle" was a term revered by the entire nation.

23. Jean Lacouture, *Ho Chi Minh: A Political Biography* (New York: Random House, 1968), 78.

24. "Reconstitutive rhetoric" is rhetorical discourse that attempts to "reform anew" or reconstitute listeners into a new way of thinking that might allow them to think for

themselves, or rather as themselves. This form of rhetorical discourse consists of the second persona, or that which is perceived as the "ideal auditor" established by the rhetor; the first persona; and substantive themes and arguments presented by the rhetor. See Frederick J. Antczak, *Thought and Character: The Rhetoric of Democratic Education* (Ames: Iowa State University Press, 1985), 9.

25. Background information is taken from the "Summary Biography of President Ho Chi Minh," *Vietnam Courier* (8 September 1969).

26. John C. Hammerback, "Jose Antonio's Rhetoric of Fascism," *Southern Journal of Communication* 3 (1994), 183.

27. Ibid.

28. David L. Hall and Roger T. Ames, *Thinking through Confucius* (Albany: State University of New York Press, 1987), 324.

29. Ibid.

30. One cannot understand Vietnamese culture without first learning about Chinese culture, hence the "Sino/Vietnamese" connotations.

31. Hall and Ames, *Thinking through Confucius*, 326.

32. Ibid.

33. Ibid., 328.

34. Glen Fisher, *International Negotiation: A Cross-Cultural Perspective* (Washington, D.C.: Library of Congress, Intercultural Press, 1980), 7.

35. Fisher, *International Negotiation: A Cross-Cultural Perspective*, 7.

36. Tran Van Dinh, "The Rhetoric of Revolt: Ho Chi Minh as Communicator," *Journal of Communication* 26, no. 4 (Autumn 1976), 142–147. See also Hue-Tam, *Radicalism and the Origins of the Vietnamese Revolution*, 254–257.

37. See Antczak, *Thought and Character*.

2

Biographical Account

Wearily to the wood the birds fly seeking rest.
Across the empty sky a lonely cloud is drifting.
In a village in the mountains, a young girl grinds out maize.
When the maize is all ground, the fire burns red in the oven.[1]

The keystone to Ho Chi Minh's persona, and in part, the success of his rhetorical discourse, originates with his early education and childhood. The name Ho Chi Minh is one of many pseudonyms. Unlike Mao Tse-tung, Ho never described his early life and political development to a Western observer.[2] For details of his family history, childhood, and youth, we are dependent exclusively on secondhand or thirdhand information published in Hanoi.

Ho's native province was traditionally a source of nationalistic ideas. The members of his own family were not people to accept the fate of their country as immutable. Some of them were actively involved in some form of a resistance movement against the French. Ho was born Nguyen Sinh Cung on 19 May 1890,[3] a descendent from a long line of brilliant scholars, who were, for the most part, junior mandarins and minor landlords.[4] His paternal grandfather, Nguyen Sinh, was a trained mandarin, a man of integrity who had earned the title of *Cu Nhan* (Master of Arts),[5] and was appointed a district governor.[6] His father, Nguyen Sinh Sac (or Huy),[7] was the son of a concubine rather than a first wife and, thus, was considered lower on the social scale than his elder half brothers. Nevertheless, Sinh Sac did manage to attend the village school and later became a man of letters and a mandarin like his father, and was conferred the title of *Pho Bang* (Doctorate of Classical Humanities).[8] He eventually took a post as a secretary in the Ministry of Protocol, in Hue, but was later dismissed for having "nationalist leanings."[9]

There is no date recorded for the death of Ho's mother, but it is known that she died very early in his life, around the age of ten. At the time of his mother's death, Ho lived with her; his father was living 350 miles north of the village in Thanh Hoa where he had been sent by his government. Therefore, Ho went to live with his grandparents and was raised by them. Ho's sister and older brother, natural siblings from same parents, were active in the various resistance movements against the French.[10] As for Ho, he passed his *certificat d'etudes primaires* in 1907 and was appointed a teacher in an elementary school, where he taught French and *quoc ngu*[11] until September 1911.[12] There is only sketchy information for the period 1911–1916 because Ho rarely talked about that period of his life.[13] Whole years present us with an almost total blank. There is no major political figure of the twentieth century about whose early life we know so little as we do about Ho's.[14]

> Only when out on the road can we take stock of our dangers.
> After we climb one mountain, another looms into view:
> But, once we have struggled up to the top of the mounta in range,
> More than ten thousand li can be surveyed at a glance.[15]

Economic necessity, allied with his inability to adjust to life under colonial rule and the urge to meet the challenge of unfamiliar cultures, compelled Ho to join the crew (under the alias Ba[16]) of the *Admiral Latouche-Treville* of the *Compagnie des Chargeurs Reunis*, a liner in service on the Haiphong–Marseilles run, as a kitchen helper.[17] The two years that Ho spent on the *Latouche-Treville* gave him a far more comprehensive education than any he might have obtained within the walls of a university. Promoted to cook's helper, Ho had ample time at sea to read Shakespeare, Tolstoy, Marx, and other great shakers (writers and leaders of major social movements) of the world.[18] Visiting Africa, Europe, Australia, and South and North America, he went ashore at all of the principal ports: Oran, Dakar, Diego-Suarez, Port Said, and Alexandria, where he observed conditions closely akin to those in Vietnam, and his findings were to constitute the factual basis of his first book *Le Proces de la colonisation francaise*, an indict-ment of France's entire colonial record.[19] On one of his trips to North America, he debarked in New York and visited Harlem. It was there that he observed, or, more correctly, read about, the conditions of American Negroes and lynching, "a little-known aspect of American civilization," which he later wrote about in an indignant article printed in *La Correspondence Internationale*.[20] During his two years at sea he worked hard to develop his effectiveness as an international revolutionary.[21] Although he wrote continually, the output was either journalism or polemics; there are no diaries[22] and almost no surviving letters.[23]

Toward the end of 1913, after roughly two years seafaring, Ho went ashore at Le Havre[24] and ended his career as a seaman.[25] Shortly thereafter, he crossed the Channel and found work in London.[26] At first he eked out a living washing dishes and shoveling snow.[27] With his ability to speak French as well as English (which he learned during his time at sea), he soon found employment at the posh Carlton Hotel and quickly gained the favor of the incomparable Escoffier, who soon promoted him to the pastry division, a choice spot.[28]

It was during this time that Ho decided to join a clandestine organization of Oriental expatriates, the Lao Dong Hoi Nagai (Overseas Workers Association).[29] This was the first time since he became an adult that he made contact with a formal political group, albeit Chinese dominated.[30] He also took an intense interest in the Irish uprising, mingled with Fabians, and read books on politics—from which he learned the meaning of the word "revolution."[31]

What exactly happened next is lost in mythology and hagiography. Ho's close associate Prime Minister Pham Van Dong says in a small pamphlet published in 1961 that Ho again returned to sea during the early part of World War I, which would be clearly consistent with the then prevailing situation: wartime food restrictions made pastry cooks a premium on the market, but high shipping losses due to the kaiser's U-boats put a premium (as well as premium wages) on men who were willing to go to sea.[32] Thus, the record of his years at sea is limited almost to the bald statement that "he went to France, then round Africa, to England and America, visiting many countries in Europe."[33]

But Truong Chinh's 1966 version of the facts asserts that Ho, upon learning that France was shipping almost one hundred thousand Indochinese (mostly Vietnamese) to France, immediately went to France to spread his nationalist views among them.[34] He feared that they would either replace French manpower in the war plants or, like the British Indians on the Somme or the French Senegalese at Verdun, serve in the trenches. Ho realized that nothing he did in London could have much influence on his country's future.[35] And despite the war and the fact that the Annamese were subject to the draft, Ho made his way to Paris in the darkest days of 1917—a few weeks before the Bolsheviks seized control of the Winter Palace in Petrograd and Lenin set up the dictatorship of the proletariat.[36]

> The cocks crow once, the night is not yet over.
> Slowly the moon climbs up the autumn hills
> In company with the stars, but now the traveller
> Who journeys far is already out on the road;
> His face is beaten with icy gusts of wind.[37]

The France Ho discovered on 3 December 1917[38] seemed altogether different from the France—oppressor of his country—that he knew in the East.[39] Here was a nation at war, menaced on all sides and swept by powerful revolutionary currents.[40] Now, for the first time, he had contact with people in metropolitan France and found their behavior and beliefs quite different from the French he had met in the colonies.[41] It was as if they were two different breeds: the right-wing, race-conscious Frenchmen who served their nation overseas, and the other French at home, far less prejudiced.[42] All around him during this period he saw the deprivation of the average French workingman, and it was a revelation: before this, he believed that all Frenchmen were rich and powerful, all Asians weak and poor.[43] Now he was looking at frightened and hungry Frenchmen, and they seemed less aware of racial distinctions.[44]

In Paris he took a new name. Readopting his patronymic of Nguyen he added Ai Quoc, meaning "love one's country"; in other words, Nguyen the Patriot. This was to be the name that for fifteen years filled an ever-expanding file in the French Sûreté (police security).[45]

You are only a very ordinary cock,
But every morning you crow to announce the dawn
Cock-a-doodle-do! You rouse the people from sleep.
Truly your daily job is not unimportant.[46]

Ho began his lengthy campaign for Vietnamese independence immediately after the end of World War I, when he founded "The League of Vietnamese Patriots Residing in Paris," and his first political action was an eight-point memorandum, demanding freedom and self-determination for the "small nation" of Vietnam,[47] which he presented to the representatives of the great powers convening at Versailles: the United States, Great Britain, France, and Germany.[48] Ho was one of a large number of representatives of subject nations who demanded that the victorious Allied powers should recognize their claims to independence and self-government in accordance with President Woodrow Wilson's principles of "self-determination for small nations."[49] Unsuccessful at Versailles, Ho remained in Paris, and through his contacts with other Vietnamese patriots, he soon got to know several important French left-wing intellectuals who not only treated him as an equal but even made much of him.[50] The reason for this was not only that this poetical-looking Asiatic won their minds and hearts but that during the war "Overseas France" had taken on a new significance: France had become dependent on its resources, and in order to secure the cooperation of the colonies, all French political groups tended to woo them.[51] The Socialists were thus encouraged to favor all their Asiatic comrades.[52] Ho met trade union officials and pacifists, wrote articles for *L'Humanite* under the title "Reminiscences of an Exile," and wrote a political play called *The Bamboo Dragon*.[53] He met Marx's grandson, and became the first Vietnamese member of the Young Socialists.[54] By 1921 the turbulence of the revolutionary wave had subsided. President Wilson, satisfied that at least some small nations had won "self-determination," shook the dust of Europe from his feet and returned home to find that his compatriots now had their eyes firmly fixed on the Pacific Ocean and the islands and lands that lay to the Far West.[55]

William Warby noted that this half-decade (from 1917 to 1921) was the most revolutionary period in man's history.[56] During these few years, great masses of ordinary people—workers, peasants, and artisans—for the first time were caught in the toils of total war and total revolution, and were educated by events as they had never been by fifty years of preaching and teaching from radical intellectuals. During this period were created the new institutions and organizations that were to dominate the social and political developments of the modern world.

During these five revolutionary years, Paris was at the center of events and of all the new cultural, intellectual, and political currents that they animated.[57] Ho was there during this period, absorbing events and ideas at a rapid rate and responding to them with equal alacrity. He became one of the founding members of the French Communist Party,[58] copublished the revolutionary *Le Paria* (an organ of the intercolonial Union), and started another publication called *Viet*

Nam Hon (the Soul of Vietnam), which was aimed at sympathizers outside of France.[59] Ho also wrote his first major contribution to revolutionary literature: *Le Proces de la Colonisation Francaise,* a treatise of some thirty thousand words, and also wrote for *La Vie Ouvriere* (Working Class Life).[60] A biting account of French repression is recounted in an article Ho wrote about the French fierceness of repression: "If the French colonists are unskillful in developing colonial resources, they are masters in the art of savage repression and the manufacture of loyalty made to measure. The Ghandis and the De Valeras would have long since entered heaven had they been born in one of the French colonies."[61]

Ho's early writings not only denounced colonialism, they also enunciated the sustained hardships and inequities of Vietnamese life, and recounted the injustices committed on the Vietnamese people by the French sovereignty.[62] "Annamese Peasant Conditions," published in *La Vie Ouvriere*, which had a distribution that included Europe, Africa, and Asia, offered an acerbic account of these injustices: "One can see that behind a mask of democracy, French imperialism has transplanted in Annam the whole cursed medieval regime . . . and that the Annamese peasantry is crucified on the bayonet of capitalist civilization and on the cross of prostituted Christianity."[63] By 1922 Ho was accepted as something of an expert on matters concerned with the Far East.[64]

By the end of this period his basic political education was complete. His small voice at Versailles, speaking on behalf of a country known only to its native inhabitants and a few French capitalists, officers, and colonial officials, had been drowned out in the babble of European suitors.[65] From this experience and from the events of the succeeding years he drew his conclusions, fixed his targets, and planned his strategy.[66] The only people who understood what was happening in Asia and Africa and who had offered practical help were in Moscow.[67] For Ho the road to Moscow was the beginning of the road back to Vietnam.

> Nine days of ceaseless rain for one day of fine weather!
> Really the sky above must be a pitiless thing.
> My shoes are in pieces, the muddy road soils my feet,
> But however it is done I have to keep on moving.[68]

In mid-1923[69] Ho went to Russia as a representative of the French colonies at the International Peasants' Congress (*Krestintern*).[70] After the congress he remained in Moscow and was a member of the first group of Vietnamese to study Marxism at the University of the Toilers of the East.[71] Late in 1924, Ho arrived in Canton, China.[72] Ostensibly, he had been sent from Moscow to be an interpreter for the Comintern mission to the Kuomintang (better known as the KMT—the Chinese Nationalist Party),[73] however, his real task was the introduction of Communism into Vietnam.[74] The day he set out for China marked the beginning of another period of his revolutionary career.

Thahn-Nien ("Youth") is the abbreviation of the term *Viet-Nam Thanh-Nien Cach-Menh Dong-Chi Hoi* (the Association of Vietnamese Revolutionary Young Comrades).[75] This was the name that Ho gave to a crypto-Communist organization that he founded in Canton in 1925.[76] Ho made himself known as Lee Suei (Ly Thuy in Vietnamese spelling) to the Chinese authorities, to whom he passed himself off as a Chinese national.[77] But to the Vietnamese he met in Canton, he admitted to being a compatriot and asked them to call him Vuong Son Nhi or Mr. Vuong. It is significant that at this early stage of his revolutionary career Ho had yet to acquire discretion. In inventing two names for himself, he had been unable to resist playing a Chinese word game prevalent at the time among Chinese and Vietnamese scholars.[78] The game consisted of splitting the ideogram representing one's own name into its component parts, each part being an ideogram by itself, and then using these parts as a pseudonym. In this case the character *Suei* (pronounced Twee in Vietnamese) is made up of the three characters *Vuong, Son,* and *Nhi.* This slight indiscretion enabled the better-educated Vietnamese—and many Vietnamese émigrés were highly educated—to discern at once that Ly Thuy and Vuong Son Nhi were one and the same person. The next time he visited the same area (in 1941) he was far more careful to keep his identity a secret, which is indicative of his greater maturity.[79]

Early in 1925 Ho formed an inner Communist group called *Thanh Nien Cong San Doan* (Communist Youth League) within Thanh Nien. One of the organization's most important functions, and according to Thomas Hodgkin "perhaps *the* most important function,"[80] was the production of the journal *Thanh Nien,* which was widely distributed throughout Northern Vietnam, Laos, and Thailand. It had a longer life than *Le Paria* and, like *Le Paria,* survived the withdrawal of its creator and principal editor and contributor Ho Chi Minh.[81] It continued on a weekly basis until April 1927 when Chiang Kai-shek carried out his counterrevolutionary coup and massacre of Kwangtung Communists and Ho escaped to Moscow.[82]

By the time of his return to Hong Kong in 1930,[83] almost three years later, a new phase of history had been reached. In the interim, Ho spent his time wandering, under the general direction of the Comintern, returning briefly to Moscow from China; reestablishing contact with the University of the Toiling Peoples of the East;[84] moving on to Berlin, Paris, and Brussels (for the 1928 Congress against Imperialist War); then to Italy, via Switzerland; and finally he boarded a Japanese ship to Thailand.[85]

From autumn 1928 until the end of 1929, Ho stayed in northeast Thailand, using the name Thau Chin and dressing as a bonze. He worked with the important Vietnamese community in this region through a broadly based organization called *Hoi Thanh Ai Nguoi Annam O Xiem* (Friendly Society of Vietnamese in Siam), which supported a school where Thai and Vietnamese were taught side by side, and a newspaper *Thanh Ai* (Friendship).[86]

> Having climbed over steep mountains and high peaks,
> How should I expect on the plains to meet greater danger?
> In the mountains, I met the tiger and came out unscathed.
> On the plains, I encountered men, and was thrown into prison.[87]

On 5 June 1931, the man who was a "master of the art of conspiracy for the sake of the party"[88] was arrested for the first time by the British in Hong Kong,[89] who were honoring a French Sûreté extradition request. As a result, the Comintern's Far Eastern Bureau was broken up, and the Vietnamese party's contacts with Moscow were disrupted.[90] While Ho was in prison rumors circulated that he had died of "advanced tuberculosis" in British custody in 1931.[91] The last entry made in the Hanoi Sûreté reads: "died in Hong Kong prison, 1933."[92] His death was authenticated by *L'Humanite* and the Soviet press.[93]

In July 1932 Frank Loseby, an anti-imperialist lawyer and British citizen, appeared, on Ho's behalf, before the Privy Council by Sir Stafford Cripps in Hong Kong.[94] After the successful defense, he managed to get Ho out of a British hospital and hide him in Amoy, where he stayed for six months.[95] According to Nguyen Luong Bang, Ho resumed his political activities in Shanghai in the early days of 1933.[96] In 1934 he eventually found his way by train to Moscow, where he stayed for some three years.[97] During this time Ho never lost touch with his own Indochinese Communist Party (ICP). From Moscow, he regularly dispatched articles on doctrine to *Tin Tuc* (The News), the ICP's official organ in Saigon.[98]

In August 1938 Ho returned to China where the Japanese threat had compelled Chiang Kai-shek to re-ally with the Communists in order to fight the invader.[99] The general staff of the Kuonmintang asked the Chinese Communist Party for instructors to teach its troops guerrilla tactics.[100] Ho found himself indoctrinating Chiang Kai-shek's troopers—just as Chou En-Lai had done ten years earlier at the Kuonmintang's Whampoa Military Academy.

Ho finally returned to Vietnam, arriving in Cao Bang in February 1941; this was his first visit to Vietnam in nearly three decades.[101] After a thorough analysis of both the national and the international situations, Ho called a meeting of Vietnamese Communist cadres. Thus, the Eighth Plenum of the ICP Central Committee, the most important meeting that outlined the course of the resistance war, was held in the Pac Bo grottoes[102] from 10 May to 19 May, 1941. Ho, "who then represented the Communist International, was in the chair."[103] With a view to bringing all resistance elements under his control, winning power, then eliminating nationalist competitors and creating a Communist state, Ho decided to form a united front whose announced program would be to coordinate all nationalist activities, drive out the French and Japanese Fascists, regain national independence, and build a Democratic Republic of Vietnam.[104] Thus was founded the Viet Nam Doc Lap Dong Minh Hoi (Vietnam Independence League), popularly known thereafter as the Vietminh.[105]

> People who come out of prison can build up the country.
> Misfortune is a test of people's fidelity.
> Those who protest at injustice are people of true merit.
> When the prison doors are opened, the real dragon will fly out.[106]

On a rainy day in August 1942, Ho set out on another journey to China, this time he sought to enlist the support of the Kuonmintang.[107] Contrary to his expectation, the Kuonmintang, which had broken with the Communists and looked with disfavor on the Vietminh activities in both China and Vietnam, coldly rejected his proposal. Worse still, on 28 August 1942, he was arrested and imprisoned on a charge that he was a French spy.[108] Not only had the Vietminh cadre learned of their mentor's misfortune, but news soon followed that Ho died while imprisoned. For several months, his presumed death had been accepted as a reality until one day his comrades received a newspaper mailed from China that contained, in its margin, a short but optimistic poem in the old revolutionary's own handwriting.[109]

Because the Japanese occupied French colonial territories, the Chinese were unable to obtain what it needed most: reports on Japanese troop movements in Indochina.[110] Sensing the Chinese dilemma, Ho,[111] who was still in prison, struck a bargain with General Chiang Fa-ku'ei: He offered to place his intelligence organization at the general's disposal in return for his release.[112] Consequently, the Chinese government welcomed the offer, and on 16 September 1943, Ho was freed.[113]

In November 1944, after Ho had slipped back into Tonkin, the British dropped supplies to Free French and Vietminh guerrillas in the border provinces. By this time Ho enjoyed the support of the Allied powers and the Vietnamese.[114] By the winter of 1944–1945, the Vietminh movement had spread throughout northern Tonkin.[115] And when the Japanese military authorities took over full power on 9 March 1945, the French plans to destroy the weak Vietminh guerrilla units in a rapid campaign were thwarted.[116]

By the spring of 1945, the Japanese hold in Indochina had begun to disintegrate. Both the nationalists and the Communists began to assert their authority throughout the southern area.[117] The dropping of the atom bomb on Hiroshima[118] on 6 August 1945, the Soviet declaration of war and attack on Manchuria during the night and early morning of 8 and 9 August, and the atom bomb dropped on Nagasaki on 9 August shattered Tokyo's resolve.[119] On 10 August, Japan declared itself ready to surrender.[120]

On 19 August 1945, five days after the Japanese surrendered to the Allies, the Vietminh captured undefended Hanoi.[121] Emperor Bao Dai abdicated in favor of Ho who proclaimed himself President of the Provincial Government of the Democratic Republic of Vietnam.[122] It was not until 2 September 1945, in Hanoi, that Ho Chi Minh declared the independence of the Democratic Republic of Vietnam.[123] This declaration was fashioned after the Declaration of the United States of America and the Declaration of the French Revolution in 1791 on the Rights of Man and the Citizen.[124] This was an extremely important event in world history—perhaps the most important event since the 1917 October Revolution in Russia.[125] It marked the first occasion in history in which a revolutionary national movement under Communist leadership had succeeded in overthrowing the power of a colonial state and establishing and maintaining its own new, independent form of social and political system.[126] For the first time in eighty-three years, a Vietnamese government had been in a position to direct the affairs of the entire country in complete independence.[127]

In less than two weeks, the northern and central sections of Vietnam were almost entirely in Communist hands.[128] This was not the case, however, in the southern region. Ho's new government did not have a dominant role in the newly established "Committee for the South."[129] And it was here that the euphoria of national self-determination failed to be realized. The commander of the British expeditionary forces, General Douglas Gracey, was sympathetic to the restoration of French colonial rule. In defiance of the agreement at Potsdam,[130] which stated that the Allied forces would avoid intervention in the local political situation of Vietnam, Gracey disarmed the Vietminh[131] and other nationalist groups and turned power over to the French, whose military units began to arrive in October 1945.[132] For months, the French- and Communist-dominated government in Hanoi attempted to avoid war. During the fall of 1946, it became increasingly apparent that war could not be avoided, and on 19 December 1946, the first Indochina war began.[133]

NOTES

1. Ho Chi Minh, *Prison Diary*, trans. Aileen Palmer (Hanoi: Foreign Languages Publishing House, 1966). Because the original date has never been verified, each author postulates the approximate date. Even Ho never publicly stated exact dates.

2. Reinhold Neumann-Hoditz, *Portrait of Ho Chi Minh: An Illustrated Biography*, trans. John Hargreaves (Hamburg: Herder and Herder, 1972), 19.

3. Cung means "respectful." He kept this name until the age of ten when, according to the prevailing practice of the time, he was given another name, Nguyen Tat Thanh ("Nguyen Who Will Inevitably Succeed"). The date of his birth is now given in official records.

4. Hoang Van Chi, *From Colonialism to Communism: A Case History of North Vietnam* (New York: Frederick A. Praeger, 1964), 36.

5. N. Khac Huyen, *Vision Accomplished? The Enigma of Ho Chi Minh* (New York: Macmillan, 1971), 3.

6. Hoang, *From Colonialism to Communism: A Case History of North Vietnam*, 36.

7. Nguyen Sinh Sac also enthusiastically participated in open guerrilla warfare against the French around 1884–1885 when a new young Vietnamese emperor, Nam-Nghi, ascended to the throne in 1884 and led his own government officials against the French. The French dubbed this *la Revolte des Lettres* (the Intellectuals' Rebellion), which they succeeded in crushing in 1888. See Bernard Fall, *Last Reflections on a War* (Garden City, N.Y.: Doubleday, 1967), 63.

8. Jean Lacouture, *Ho Chi Minh: A Political Biography* (New York: Random House, 1968), 14.

9. Neumann-Hoditz, *Portrait of Ho Chi Minh: An Illustrated Biography*, 22–23.

10. Charles Fenn, *Ho Chi Minh: A Biographical Introduction* (New York: Charles Scribner's Sons, 1973), 17.

11. Ho was trained in the Confucian tradition, along with reading and writing Chinese ideograms, and was sent to a public school to study *quoc ngu* and French. See Huyen, *Vision Accomplished? The Enigma of Ho Chi Minh*, 4. *Quoc ngu* is the Vietnamese language that was Romanticized by the Jesuit missionary Alexandre de Rhodes, who replaced the ideographs with the Latin alphabet in 1627.

12. William J. Duiker writes that the influence of the father on the son was significant because Nguyen Sinh Sac had come to detest the traditional system of education, even though he had profited from it. He became a wandering scholar, he often deprecated the civil service system and the old literature, and he vowed that he would never teach his own children to follow that route. Young Ho understandably applauded his father's attitude. See William J. Duiker, *The Rise of Nationalism in Vietnam, 1900–1941* (Ithaca, N.Y.: Cornell University Press, 1976), 94–95.

13. William Warby, *Ho Chi Minh and the Struggle for an Independent Vietnam* (London: Merlin, 1972), 19.

14. Fenn, *Ho Chi Minh: A Biographical Introduction*, 25.

15. Minh, *Prison Diary*.

16. Ho changed his name from Cung to Ba presumably because the French Sûreté police already had him listed under his own name. See Charles Fenn, *Ho Chi Minh: A Biographical Introduction* (New York: Charles Scribner's Sons, 1973), 23.

17. The *Compagnie des Chargeurs Reunis* plied between Indo-China and its home port of Marseilles, with innumerable calls en route according to cargo requirements. The term *"Chargeurs"* suggests that the ships were essentially freighters, although there would also have been passengers—first, second, third, and even fourth class—crowding every inch of space. The job of kitchen helper would not have called for any qualifications because the designation "assistant cook, cook's helper, kitchen helper," covers all those unskilled workers who peel potatoes, scrub out the galley, and run and fetch between the storeroom and the pantry. See Fenn, *Ho Chi Minh*, 23–24. See also Lacouture, *Ho Chi Minh*, 17.

18. Jules Archer, *Ho Chi Minh: Legend of Hanoi* (Folkestone, U.K.: Bailey Brothers and Swinfen, 1971), 6.

19. Lacouture, *Ho Chi Minh*, 18.

20. Huyen, *Vision Accomplished?*, 6.

21. Archer, *Ho Chi Minh*, 6.

22. *Prison Diary*, which consists of poems expressing emotions rather than facts, is the only known existing diary attributed to Ho Chi Minh. See Minh, *Prison Diary*.

23. Fenn, *Ho Chi Minh*, 25.

24. Historians disagree whether Ho went back to sea shortly before World War I. Some accounts have him back at sea shortly before the war, while others assert that when he debarked in Le Havre, he never returned to sea as a crew hand.

25. Fenn, *Ho Chi Minh*, 26.

26. David Halberstam, *Ho* (New York: Random House, 1971), 26.

27. Lacouture, *Ho Chi Minh*, 18.

28. Fall, *Last Reflections on a War*, 66.

29. Halberstam, *Ho*, 26.

30. That association, though ostensibly concerned with improving the working conditions of foreign workers excluded from the local labor unions, had also begun to address itself to the problem of political organization of its members once they returned to their respective homelands. As the later histories of nationalist movements in British

colonies clearly show, those overseas workers' associations, by virtue of the fact that they were dealing with a compact urban audience generally protected by the laws of free assembly which willy-nilly applied to them in Britain and France (but not in British India or French Indochina), became an important adjunct to the eventual liberation of their homelands. See Fall, *Last Reflections on a War,* 66.

31. Lacouture, *Ho Chi Minh,* 18.

32. Fall, *Last Reflections on a War,* 66.

33. *Days with Ho Chi Minh* (Hanoi: Foreign Languages Publishing House, 1965), 38.

34. In the case of Ho, both Chinh's and Prime Minister Dong's accounts are, in fact, not mutually exclusive. There is strong circumstantial evidence that Ho *did* return to sea on the deadly transatlantic wartime runs, visiting Boston, New York, and other East and Gulf Coast ports, because he later wrote vivid accounts of what Dong calls "the barbarities and ugliness of American capitalism, the Ku Klux Klan mobs, the lynching of Negroes." A pamphlet written by Ho in Moscow in 1924 entitled *La Race Noire* seems to be based in part on what he heard and saw in the United States during his trips in 1914–1916. But there is no question that he moved to France in early 1917 and that his motives were political, this time. See Fall, *Last Reflections on a War,* 67.

35. Lacouture, *Ho Chi Minh,* 19.

36. Ibid.

37. Minh, *Prison Diary.*

38. Archer, *Ho Chi Minh,* 9.

39. Lacouture, *Ho Chi Minh,* 19.

40. Ibid.

41. Halberstam, *Ho,* 27.

42. Ibid.

43. Ibid.

44. Ibid.

45. Fenn, *Ho Chi Minh,* 27.

46. Minh, *Prison Diary.*

47. Warby, *Ho Chi Minh,* 24.

48. John T. McAlister Jr. and Paul Mus, *The Vietnamese and Their Revolution* (New York: Harper and Row, 1970), 67.

49. Warby, *Ho Chi Minh,* 24.

50. Fenn, *Ho Chi Minh,* 27.

51. Ibid.

52. Ibid.

53. Halberstam, *Ho,* 28.

54. Ibid.

55. Warby, *Ho Chi Minh,* 25.

56. Ibid.

57. Ibid.

58. Halberstam, *Ho,* 35.

59. Fenn, *Ho Chi Minh,* 28.

60. Ibid.

61. Ho Chi Minh, "Some Considerations on the Colonial Question," *L'Humanite* (May 25, 1922).

62. Ho Chi Minh, "Annamese Women and French Domination," *Le Paria* 1922; located in the Indochina Archives, University of California–Berkeley. Also refer to Ho Chi

Minh, "Indochina and the Pacific," *La Correspondence Internationale* 18 (1924) and "The Failure of French Colonization," *La Correspondence Internationale* 26 (1924).

63. Ho Chi Minh, "Annamese Peasant Conditions," *La Vie Ouvriere* (January 4, 1924).

64. Fenn, *Ho Chi Minh*, 28.

65. Warby, *Ho Chi Minh*, 25.

66. Ibid.

67. Ibid.

68. Minh, *Prison Diary*.

69. Hoang Van Chi joined the Vietminh sometime shortly after World War II, where he remained until the defeat of the French in 1954. Accordingly, Hoang states that Ho's first visit to Russia was in 1922, as a first colonial delegate to the Fourth Congress of the Communist International, returning in 1923 to attend the Peasant's International Congress and again in 1924 to become a student at the Eastern Workers' University, where he remained for more than one year before going to Canton, China, in 1925. See Hoang, *From Colonialism to Communism*, 40. William Warby places Ho in Moscow in the winter of 1923, shortly before the death of Lenin. Warby also writes that *Pravda*, on 27 January 1924, published a moving tribute written by Ho when he heard the news of Lenin's death. See Warby, *Ho Chi Minh*, 32.

70. Duiker, *Rise of Nationalism*, 199. See also *Ho Chi Minh and the Communist Movement in Indo-China: A Study in the Exploitation of Nationalism* (located in the Indochina Archives, University of California, Berkeley, file DRV, Subj BIOG, date August 1953, Sub-cat Ho Chi Minh), 5.

71. S.R. Mohan Das, *Ho Chi Minh—Nationalist or Soviet Agent?* (Bombay: R. Swarup, 1950), 2.

72. There is some disagreement over his arrival date. Some biographers place Ho in China in December 1924; others place him there in early 1925. The more notable biographers accept the earlier date. See Duiker, *Rise of Nationalism*, 199.

73. Ibid.

74. Hoang, *From Colonialism to Communism*, 42.

75. The word *Dong Chi* (in Chinese *T'ung Chi*), which means "comrade," reflects the communist tendency of the movement. This is the first occasion of its use in the Vietnamese language. See Hoang, *From Colonialism to Communism*, 41.

76. Ibid.

77. Ibid., 42.

78. Ibid.

79. Ibid.

80. Thomas Hodgkin, *Vietnam: The Revolutionary Path* (London: Macmillan, 1981), 224–225.

81. Ibid.

82. Ibid.

83. Thomas Hodgkin places him in Hong Kong on this date (*Vietnam*, 225–226); Hoang Van Chi places him in Hong Kong at the end of 1929 (*From Colonialism to Communism*); and Reinhold Neumann-Hoditz asserts that he may have been on the Chinese mainland during this period: "Even his closest comrades did not know the answer" (*Portrait of Ho Chi Minh*, 110).

84. According to Hodgkin, Ho reestablished old ties with a former friend and colleague, Le Hong Phong, who was influential in the early days of the Vietnamese Communist movement (*Vietnam*, 228).

85. Ibid., 228.

86. Ibid., 228–229.

87. Minh, *Prison Diary.*

88. *Pravda* wrote about Ho as such.

89. Neumann-Hoditz, *Portrait of Ho Chi Minh*, 112–113.

90. Duiker, *Rise of Nationalism*, 230.

91. Neumann-Hoditz, *Portrait of Ho Chi Minh*, 120–121.

92. Lacouture, *Ho Chi Minh*, 34.

93. Ibid.

94. Neumann-Hoditz, *Portrait of Ho Chi Minh*, 118.

95. Lacouture, *Ho Chi Minh*, 69.

96. Ibid.

97. Warby, *Ho Chi Minh*, 40.

98. Lacouture, *Ho Chi Minh*, 69.

99. Jean Sainteny, *Ho Chi Minh and His Vietnam: A Personal Memoir* (Chicago: Cowles Book Company, 1972), 28.

100. Lacouture, *Ho Chi Minh*, 70.

101. Huyen, *Vision Accomplished?*, 51.

102. According to Jean Chesneaux, Philippe Devilers, Donald Lancaster, and Le Thanh Khoi, the meeting took place in the little Chinese village of Tsingtsi. Communist sources, however, put it at Pac Bo, a remote village in the province of Cao Bang, Tonkin. See Jean Chesneaux, *The Vietnamese Nation: Contribution to a History* (Sydney: Current Book Distributors, 1966), 155.

103. Truong Chinh, *President Ho Chi Minh: Beloved Leader of the Vietnamese People* (Hanoi: Foreign Languages Publishing House, 1966), 24.

104. Huyen, *Vision Accomplished?*, 53.

105. It should be noted that the term "Vietminh" is composed of the first and last words of Viet-Nam Doc Lap Dong Minh (Vietnam Independence League), or the abbreviation of the name of that organization, which was a national movement for independence including Communists and non-Communist elements. The term "Vietminh" does not mean Vietnamese Communists as foreign reporters and authors usually understand.

106. Minh, *Prison Diary*, 32.

107. Huyen, *Vision Accomplished?*, 58.

108. Neumann-Hoditz, *Portrait of Ho Chi Minh*, 136.

109. Huyen, *Vision Accomplished?*, 58.

110. Ibid., 62.

111. It must be remembered that Ho Chi Minh was not his name at this time, it was still Nguyen Ai Quoc, the same Nguyen Ai Quoc who had confronted the powers at the Treaty of Versailles. The reputation of Nguyen Ai Quoc, the shrewd agent of international Communism, certainly made him a persona non grata to Chungking, which kept a copious dossier on him. To overcome this difficulty, the Vietnamese Communist once again changed his name from Nguyen Ai Quoc to Ho Chi Minh—He Who Enlightens.

112. Huyen, *Vision Accomplished?*, 62.

113. Ibid., 63.

114. Ibid., 67.

115. Neumann-Hoditz, *Portrait of Ho Chi Minh*, 143.

116. Ibid., 146.

117. Douglas Pike, *Viet Cong* (Cambridge: MIT Press, 1966), 28.

118. Stein Tonnesson, *The Vietnamese Revolution of 1945: Roosevelt, Ho Chi Minh, and de Gaulle in a World at War* (London: Sage, 1991), 396.

119. Ibid.

120. Ibid.

121. Hoang, *From Colonialism to Communism*, 60.

122. Ibid.

123. Ellen Hammer, *Vietnam: Yesterday and Today* (New York: Holt, Rinehart and Winston, 1966), 134.

124. Archimedes Patti, *Why Vietnam? Prelude to America's Albatross* (Berkeley and Los Angeles: University of California Press, 1980), 250.

125. Hodgkin, *Vietnam*, 1.

126. Ibid.

127. Chesneaux, *Vietnamese Nation*, 161.

128. William J. Duiker, *Vietnam: Nation in Revolution* (Boulder, Colo.: Westview, 1983), 40.

129. Ibid.

130. On 23 July 1945, during the Potsdam Conference, the Americans and British secured which theater of operation Indo-China belonged to. The Allies distinguished between three theaters of operation: the Pacific theater was under the direction of American General Douglas MacArthur, the Southeast Asia theater under the British Admiral Lord Mountbatten, and the Chinese theater effectively commanded by the American General Albert Wedemeyer. It was decided that the northern portion of Vietnam was in the hands of the sector that had fallen to the Chinese, and the southern portion was under British influence. The sixteenth parallel was to be the boundary between the two armies responsible for disarming the Japanese. See Jacques Dalloz, *The War in Indo-China 1945–54* (Dublin: Gill and Macmillan, 1987), 15.

131. The Eighth Plenum of the Central Committee of the Communist Party of Indochina, held at Pac Bo (Cao Bang Province) 10–19 May 1941, decided on a new line highlighting the slogan "national liberation," establishing the League of Revolutionary Organizations of Vietnam: Viet-Nam-Doc-Lap-Dong Minh-Hoi, or Vietminh for short, changing the names of various mass organizations into Associations for National Salvation. See John T. McAlister Jr., *Vietnam: The Origins of Revolution* (New York: Alfred A. Knopf, 1969), 105.

132. Duiker, *Vietnam*, 40.

133. Ibid., 42.

3

Chinese Sociocultural Influences

It would be impossible for Westerners unfamiliar with Sino/Vietnamese cultural heritage and lacking knowledge of communication methodologies, to understand and appreciate Ho Chi Minh's rhetorical power. This chapter attempts to illuminate specific aspects of traditional Chinese culture that influenced and shaped Vietnamese thought and language in order for the reader to gain a better perspective on the foundational strength of Ho's reconstitutive discourse.

Among the numerous peoples on the southern periphery of China, only the Vietnamese adopted Chinese culture without becoming a part of the Chinese political system.[1] Only in Vietnam "did the [Chinese] culture outpace the [Chinese] political unit. The Vietnamese derived their higher culture from China; and they were for a long period under Chinese rule."[2] Yet, eventually, they managed to establish their identity as a separate country within east Asian civilization.[3]

Throughout much of its history, the Vietnamese language coexisted with ancient Chinese. Indeed, it yielded to Chinese in essential fields of social life, such as government and administration, or the main fields of intellectual activity, philosophy, history, and ethics.[4]

Education figured very largely in the Vietnam of Ho's time.[5] It constituted the foundation of civic life inasmuch as it was the vehicle for the spreading of loyalist Confucian morality; it was the point of departure for all personal ambitions because the path to honors lay in the quarterly and triennial examinations; and it was publicly revered by village scholars and by the presence of numerous "Temples of Literature" in Hanoi and many other towns.[6] In old Vietnam there were perhaps twenty thousand schools where, under the guidance of elderly retired officials, children learned a few Chinese characters and the rudiments of Confucian morality. With a small stick, they traced the hallowed symbols on a board covered with soft mud, before they had the use of brush and rice paper.[7]

This chapter explores the influence that classical Chinese philosophy and Confucian ethics had on the Vietnamese culture.

A "TWO-WORLD THEORY"

The place to begin is with a description of Chinese and Western worldview assumptions. The differences between the classical Chinese worldview and those classical Greek, Roman, and Judeo–Christian assumptions that dominate and ground Western traditions are fundamental, and can be differentiated in the following terms. We can call the worldview, by the time that Plato and Aristotle had come to dominate classical Greek thinking, a "two-world theory."[8] Later, with the melding of Greek philosophy and the Judeo–Christian tradition, this "dualistic" mode of thinking became firmly entrenched in Western civilization as its dominant underlying paradigm, which is best summarized by stating that a significant concern among the most influential Greek thinkers and later the Christian Church Fathers was to discover and distinguish the world of reality from the world of change, a distinction that fostered both a two-world theory and a dualistic way of thinking about it.[9] These thinkers sought that permanent and unchanging first principle that had overcome initial chaos to give unity, order, and design to a changing world, and which they believed makes experience of this changing world intelligible to the human mind. They sought the "real" structure behind change—called variously Platonic Ideas, natural or Divine Law, moral principle, God, and so on—which, when understood, made life predictable and secure. The centrality of "metaphysics" in classical Greek philosophy, the "science" of these first principles, reflects a presumption that there is some originative and independent source of order that, when discovered and understood, will provide coherent explanation for the human experience.

According to Roger Ames, there were many diverse answers to the basic questions: What is the one behind the many? What is the unity that brings everything together as a *"universe"*? What—or who—has set the agenda that makes human life coherent, and thus meaningful? For the Jewish prophets and scribes, and later for the Christian Church Fathers, it was the existence of the one transcendent Deity who through Divine Will overcame the formless void and created the world, and in whom truth, beauty, and goodness reside. It is this One who is the permanence behind change, and who unifies our world as a single-ordered "universe." It is this One who allows for objective and universal knowledge and guarantees the truth of our understanding. Because this One is permanent and unchanging, it is more real than the chaotic world of change and appearances that it disciplines and informs. The highest kind of knowledge, then, is the discovery and contemplation (*theoria*) of what is in itself perfect, self-evident, and infallible ... "that which creates" and "that which is created," "that which orders" and "that which is ordered." What is common among these binary pairs of opposites is that the world defined by the first member is thought to stand independent of, and be superior to, the second. Because the secondary world is utterly dependent on the first, we can say that the primary world is necessary and essential, the "Being" behind the "beings," and the secondary world is only contingent and passing. There is a fundamental discontinuity in this worldview between what is real and what is less real. It is on the basis of this fundamental and pervasive distinction between a permanently real world and a changing world of appearances, then, that it can be said that our classical tradition is dominated by a two-world theory.[10]

AN IMMANENTAL COSMOS

The dominant worldview of classical China begins not from a two-world theory but from the assumption that there is only the one continuous concrete world that is the source and locus of all of our experience.[11] This precludes the existence of any transcendent being or principle. This is the presumption of radical immanence.[12] Order within the classical Chinese worldview is "immanental"—indwelling in things themselves—like the grain in wood, like striations in stone, like the cadence of the surf, like the veins in a leaf.[13] The classical Chinese believed that the power of creativity resides in the world itself, and that the order and regularity this world evidences is not derived from or imposed on it by some independent, activating power, but inheres in the world.[14] Change and continuity are equally "real."

Unlike Plato and Aristotle, the resolutely pragmatic nature of classical Chinese philosophy resists any severe distinction between theory and application and, as a consequence, philosophizing in this culture is not merely theoretical—it entails practice, "doing."[15] Being a person is something one does, not something one is; it is an achievement rather than a given.[16] The Chinese mind is primarily social.[17] The true Chinese cosmos is, monotheistic propaganda of Christian missionaries to the contrary notwithstanding, anthropocentric, never theocentric.[18] Classical Chinese philosophy entails an ontology of events, not one of substances.[19] Understanding human events does not require recourse to "qualities," "attributes," or "characteristics."[20] Thus, in place of a consideration of the essential nature of abstract moral virtues, the Chinese are more concerned with an explication of the activities of specific persons in particular contexts.[21]

The two-world order of classical Greece has given our tradition a theoretical basis for *objectivity*—the possibility of standing outside and taking a wholly external view of things.[22] Ames distinguishes between classical Greek "objectivity" and the classical Chinese "world." Objectivity allows us to decontextualize things as "objects" in our world. By contrast, in the "this world" of classical China, instead of starting abstractly from some underlying, unifying, and originating principle, we begin from our own specific place within the world. Without objectivity, objects dissolve into the flux and flow, and existence becomes a continuous, uninterrupted process. Each of us is invariably experiencing the world as one perspective within the context of many. Since there is only this world, we cannot get outside of it. From the always unique place one occupies within the continuum of Classical China, one interprets the order of the world around one as contrastive "thises" and "thats"—"this person" and "that person"—more or less proximate to oneself. Since each and every person or thing or event in the field of existence is perceived from some position that entertains it, each thing is related to and a condition of every other. All human relationships are continuous from ruler and subject to friend and friend, relating everyone as an extended "family." Similarly, all "things," like all members of a family, are correlated and interdependent. Every thing is what it is at the pleasure of everything else. Whatever can be predicted of one thing or one person is a function of a network of relationships, all of which conspire to give us its role and to constitute its place and its definition. A father is "this" good father by virtue of the quality of the relationships that locate him in this role and the deference of "these" children and "that" mother, who all sustain him in it.

Because all things are unique, there is no strict notion of identity (previously described) in the sense of some selfsame identical characteristic that makes all members of a class or category or species the same. For example, there is no essential defining feature—no divinely endowed soul, rational capacity, or natural locus of rights—that makes all human beings equal. In the absence of such equality that would make us essentially the same, the various relationships that define one thing in relation to another tend to be hierarchical and contrastive: bigger or smaller, more noble or more base, harder or softer, stronger or weaker, more senior or more junior. Change in the quality of relationships between things always occurs on a continuum as movement between polar oppositions. The general and most basic language for articulating correlations among things is metaphorical: In some particular aspect at some specific point in time, one person or one thing is "overshadowed" by another; that is, made *yin* to another's *yang*. Literally, *yin* means "shady" and *yang* means "sunny," defining in the most general terms those contrasting and hierarchical relationships that constitute indwelling order and regularity.

Ames concludes that it is important to recognize the *interdependence* and correlative character of the *yin/yang* kind of polar opposites,[23] and to distinguish this contrastive tension from the dualistic opposition implicit in the vocabulary of the classical Greek world, where one primary member of a set such as Creator stands *independent* of and is more "real" than the world he creates. The implications of this difference between dualism and polar contrast are fundamental and pervasive.[24]

Herrlee Creel supports Ames' understanding of classical Chinese thought. He states that the Chinese physical world is a world of action as opposed both to a static world and a world of substance. On the one hand, the Chinese world appears to be always in flux, to do little resting on any "eternal verities." On the other hand, we find, the Chinese world, only one sort of substance, if indeed that be a substance at all. (This is a broad generalization, and such statements may usually be shown to have exceptions. There may well be individual variations from this position, although I know of none.) Things are differentiated, not by the materials of which they are composed, but by the way in which they act. Materials pass from a state of having one sort of property to a state of having another; in the latter state they have a different name, but the only difference is one of *activity*. To the ancient thinker, the differences between things consist in degree of density (itself a kind of activity) and nature of activity.[25]

Metaphysics in the West has been presumed to be the science of order. In fact, it has most often advertised itself as the science of uniformities.[26] According to Hall and Ames, speculative philosophy—both as *scientia universalis* and as *ontologia generalis*—has sought to articulate those characteristics or relationships that allow us access to the uniformities of existence and experience. As "universal science," metaphysical speculation has uncovered those principles of order that together permit the organization and classification of the elements of the World and our experience of them.[27] The "general ontologist" searches for the meaning of the *be-ing* of beings expressed by the set of uniform relations that qualify everything that is. What is missing in Anglo-European notions of order is the *aesthetic* perspective.

Hall and Ames suggest that the aesthetic order "begins with the uniqueness of the one thing and assesses this particular as contributing to the balanced complexity of its context. Because the aesthetic celebrates the disclosure of the insistent particularity of each detail in tension with the consequent unity of these specific details, plurality must be conceived as prior to unity and disjunction as prior to conjunction. The focus of an aesthetic order is the way in which a concrete, specific detail discloses itself as producing a harmony expressed by a complex of such details in relationship to one another." They further state that the concepts of aesthetic and logical order are inversely related. Aesthetic order presses in the direction of particularity and uniqueness; logical order toward generality and absolute substitutability. Aesthetic disorder exists to the extent that there is a loss of particularity. A complex of elements reaches the maximum of aesthetic disorder with the realization of absolute uniformity. But this is the highest degree of rational *order*—concepts of "human nature," "human rights," "equality under the law," and so forth, signal the resort to logical or rational orderedness. Even the major forms of individualism are consequences of rational or logical interpretations.

A society rooted in the preference for aesthetic orderedness, assert Hall and Ames, will not be open to the employment of rules, standards, or norms that are presumed to be generalizations or instances of essential defining characteristics of human beings and of their modes of togetherness. Neither will consensus be used as objective grounds for social order. The uniformities and continuities evident within an aesthetically ordered society originate in specific acts of deference on the part of individuals whose focusing perspectives offer the variety of orders possible at any given moment.

Hall and Ames conclude, stating that in the Western tradition, belief in a single-order cosmos reinforces the search for natural and social uniformities. Laws as external determining sources of order provide the grounds for the perpetuation of a sense of rational orderedness. On the other hand, if there is little or no recourse to the concepts of a created order or a world obedient to natural laws, such order that exists must be conceived as contingent. This contingency in itself does not provide the grounds for an alternative to rational or logical order. Rules and laws, as external determining principles of order, can originate in the

arbitrariness and contingency of individual rulers, or in the inertia of unques-
tioned tradition, or in shifting patterns of consensus unthinkingly realized. The
distinctive feature of aesthetic order is that, whereas rational order permits one
to abstract from the concrete particularities of the elements of the order and to
treat these elements indifferently, aesthetic order is constituted by just those
particularities. That is to say, the variety of aesthetic orders is a function of pre-
cisely those features that distinguish one ordering perspective from another.[28]

I introduce this characterization of rational and aesthetic orders in anticipa-
tion of the treatment of Confucius' social and political theory.

CONCEPT OF REVOLUTION: THE MANDATE OF HEAVEN

The cornerstone of the ideology of the Chinese state had been the concept of
the Mandate of Heaven. This is the idea that the ruler of China held a sacred
trust from the highest deity, which permitted him to rule as long as he did so
for the welfare of the people—but subject to the peril that if he failed in this
trust, Heaven would appoint another to rebel and replace him.[29]

The cohesion and stability of the Chinese empire owes much to the almost
universal, and seldom-questioned, acceptance of the religious basis upon which
the authority of the emperor has been founded.[30] This acceptance persisted into
the twentieth century, and it comes, in unbroken line, from the beginning of
Chou.[31]

After the leaders of the Chou tribe had overthrown the Shang dynasty and
set up their own rule around 1120 B.C., they issued a number of proclamations,
preserved in the *Book of History*, explaining to the defeated Shang people why
they should submit docilely to their new conquerors.[32] In their arguments, the
Chou rulers appealed to a concept called *t'ien-ming* ("Mandate of Heaven").[33]
According to Wm. Theodore de Bary, Heaven, they said, elected or commanded
certain men to be rulers over the tribes of the world, and their heirs might continue to exercise the Heaven-sanctioned power for as long as they carried out
their religious and administrative duties with piety, wisdom, and justice. But if
the worth of the ruling family declined, if the rulers turned their backs on the
spirits and abandoned the virtuous ways that had originally marked them as
worthy of the mandate to rule, then Heaven might discard them and elect a new
family or tribe to be the destined rulers of the world. The Shang kings, it was
argued, had once been wise and benevolent rulers, and thus enjoyed the full
blessing and sanction of Heaven. But in later days they had grown cruel and de-
generate, so that Heaven had called on the Chou chieftains to overthrow the
Shangs, punish their evil ways, and institute a new dynasty.[34] Thus, the Chou
rulers explained the change of dynasties not as a purely human action by which
a strong state overthrew a weak one, but as a divinely directed process in which
a new group of wise and virtuous leaders was substituted for an old group whose
members, by their evil actions, had disqualified themselves from the right to
rule.[35]

Creel states that the Chou called their supreme ruler *Wang* (King) but they also called him "Son of Heaven." His office bestowed the highest glory possible to man. The Son of Heaven also bore the most awesome burden of responsibility. Only the continued welfare of the people could justify his continued enjoyment of his power and his title. If things went wrong, it was the duty of another to overthrow him.

Creel explains that the doctrine of the Mandate of Heaven was not merely a force imposing will work making for responsible conduct on the part of the monarch and cementing the loyalty of his vassals and officials, but it was also the central cohesive force binding together the entire Chinese people, even the humblest. This doctrine gave the Chinese individual a role in the unfolding drama of the Chinese state because it was for the people that this state had been held to exist, and no rightful government had been able to persist in the face of continued public dissatisfaction.[36] Thus, we find Confucius stating that no government can stand if it lacks the confidence of the common people,[37] and Mencius quoting with approval the saying that it is the common people who speak for heaven.[38] The people, more than any other factor, were emphasized as the key to the Mandate of Heaven.[39] The Chou had given China a vision: a world, "all under heaven," united in peace and harmony and cooperation, under "the Son of Heaven."[40]

To the Vietnamese, the Mandate of Heaven was called *Thien minh,* or the heavenly mandate.[41] Proof that a revolutionary regime had the Mandate of Heaven was the emergence of a new political system that was a complete replacement of the preceding doctrines, institutions, and men in power and that showed itself to be in complete command of society. To appear before the people—the supreme judge—with any chance of success as a messenger of fate, a revolutionary party had to show them all the signs of its mission. In this case the people expected the sign of signs: the ease and fluidity of success. The revolutionary party had to succeed in everything as if miraculously. The military and financial means were secondary considerations and would, of their own accord, put themselves in the hands of the party that had received the Mandate of Heaven.[42] Such a test of legitimacy merely indicated that the Vietnamese expected there to be little uncertainty about an insurgent's capacity to govern before there was popular recognition of his being endowed with the Mandate of Heaven. But being gamblers at heart, the Vietnamese knew that they could not wait too long, otherwise, they may lose their chance to be identified with the winning side. McAlister and Mus explain that in the critical task of making their choice the Vietnamese looked for a sign or an intimation of legitimacy, which they called *virtue.*[43] The moment a "virtue" (in the West one would say a political system) appears to be worn out and another is in view ready to take the place of the old, the previous abuses—which had been put up with until then—are seen in a new light. Then, and only then, must they be remedied with the help of a new principle. Extreme patience is thus replaced by intolerance. First the people tolerate everything; then they refuse to put up with anything. In other words, the former values do not count anymore.

This is how Vietnamese civic morality suddenly becomes intransigent.[44] Paul Mus states that it has nothing whatever to do with political pretexts. Involved here are moral values comparable to the highest in the West, but they are put into practice only when the circumstances are clearly appropriate. Such behavior derives from a centuries-old wisdom leading to civic reactions that are in no way similar to ours. Instead of going along at a moderate but continuous and slowly effective pace, the Sino/Vietnamese moral life jumps, spasmodically, from crisis to crisis far more than does that of the West.[45]

As a result, when a crisis comes, the minds of the people suddenly become susceptible to moral values and more attentive to the mistakes that have been made. They judge these errors to have been at the roots of the revolution, and, therefore, the behavior of the protagonists has a determining influence on events. It is not by accident that east Asia prefers to use the word "virtue" for what the West would call a "system."[46]

TRADITIONAL SYMBOLS OF VIETNAMESE POLITICS

Confucian moral ideal of government: "Guide the people with governmental measures and control or regulate them by the threat of punishment, and the people will try to keep out of jail, but will have no sense of honor or shame. Guide the people by virtue and control or regulate them by *li* (sense of propriety), and the people will have a sense of honor and respect."[47]

Confucius' whole system of ethics and, indeed, most of his philosophy seems to have been based on a consideration of the nature of the human being. He believed that men are to a very considerable extent (though by no means totally) made what they are by society. On the other hand, since society is nothing more than the interaction of men, society is made what it is by the individuals who compose it.[48]

Hall and Ames assert that modern social and political theory in the West has in large measure revolved around such topics as the relation of the individual to society, the realms of private and public activity, the status of natural and of positive law, the character of rights and of duties, the sanctioning power of the state (legitimate authority), the meaning of justice, and so forth. It would not be possible to employ such a list of issues in the analysis of Confucius' philosophy without distorting it beyond recognition. A representative list of subjects relevant to a discussion of Confucius' "social" and "political" theory would include a rather different set of items: the cultivation of personal life, ritual activity (*li*) as the foundation of penal law (*fa*), social roles and institutions, the ordering of names, the official as model, and so forth.

What is immediately evident from a comparison of these two lists, say Hall and Ames, is the degree to which what might be construed as distinctly ethical phenomena enter directly into reflections on social and political thinking for Confucius. The association of political order with "cultivation" and the demand that the ruler be "sage within and kingly without"—that is to say, that he can be an exemplary person (*chun tzu*)—provides a distinctly different coloration even to those topics in political theory that overlap between the Chinese and Anglo-European traditions.

The principal reason for the radical differences in problems and priorities between the Confucian and Western traditions can be accounted for in terms of the contrasting understanding or order dominating each tradition. Significant contrasts between social and political vision in Western intellectual culture and the thinking of Confucius are to be found not only in presumed differences in the procedures for realizing social order, but also in the contrasting meanings of "order."[49]

The foundation of the Vietnamese social system, like the Chinese, rested not on revealed religion but on ethics,[50] which, in part, derived from Confucianism, which had been firmly established as the "official doctrine."[51] In logical progression, Confucius rises from a discussion of duties toward the family to those toward the state, which social organization he regards as only a larger household, having all its ethical principles founded on those of the primary unit.[52] Because Confucian social theory conceived of the country as a family writ large,[53] filial piety and family harmony were the twin bases of social and political stability.[54] The various relationships that existed within the family and society were articulated by the *Three Bonds* (Virtues): loyalty (*trung;* Chinese *chung*), which a subject owed to his ruler; piety (*hieu;* Chinese *hsioa*), which governed the behavior of a son to his father; and fidelity (*nghia;* Chinese *I*), which bound husband and wife together.[55] Ideally, each of these virtues reinforced the other two. The theory of the "three virtues" (submission of subjects to kings, son to father, wife to husband) had become the moral orthodoxy.[56] The nation, the family, the person were the three levels of existence, of participation in the moral order, which mattered to the Vietnamese peasantry.[57] The regulation and good order of all three were proof that universal harmony prevailed, and that Heaven would cause the realm to prosper.[58]

THE FOUNDATION OF GOVERNMENT

This is meant by "To rightly govern the state, it is necessary first to regulate one's own family." One cannot instruct others who cannot instruct his own children. Without going beyond the family, the prince may learn all the lessons of statecraft, filial piety by which the sovereign is also served, fraternal submission by which older men and superiors are also served, kindness by which also the common people should be ministered unto.[59]

From the loving example of one family, love extends throughout the state; from its courtesy, courtesy extends throughout the state; while the ambition and perverse recklessness of one man may plunge the entire state into rebellion and disorder.[60]

By these words from "The Great Learning" the position of the family as the foundation of society and of its proper regulation as the basis for government is dwelt on. In the "Hsiao King," the application of these principles is adroitly indicated as follows: "The filial piety with which the superior man serves his parents may be transferred as loyalty to the ruler; the fraternal duty with which he serves his elder brother may be transferred as deference to elders; his regulation of his family may be transferred as good government in any official position."[61]

The strictly practical character also of this application is revealed by this saying of You Tze concerning the fount of orderly behavior on the part of the citizen: "They are few who, being filial and fraternal, are fond of offending against their superiors. There have been none who, not liking to offend against their superiors, have been fond of stirring up confusion."[62] To support and elucidate this view, also, Confucius cites the *Book of Odes* saying: "From them you learn the more immediate duty serving one's father and the remoter one of serving one's prince."[63]

And again he cites and even quotes the Shu King to show the immediate and causal relation between the exercise of filial and fraternal piety and the establishment of government on a sound and secure foundation: "What does the 'Shu King' say of filial piety? You are filial, you discharge your fraternal duties. These qualities are displayed in government. This, then, also constitutes the exercise of government."[64]

GOVERNMENT EXISTS FOR THE BENEFIT OF THE GOVERNED

"The duke of She asked about government. The Master said, 'Good government obtains when those who are near are made happy, and those who are far are attracted.'"[65] This Mencius reiterated in this direct fashion: "The people are the most important element; ... the sovereign, least important."[66] But Mencius goes far beyond that when he says to King Seuen of Ts'e: "Therefore an intelligent ruler will regulate the livelihood of the people, so as to make sure that they shall have sufficient wherewith to serve their parents and also sufficient wherewith to support their wives and children."[67]

David Marr relates this to Vietnamese culture by stating: "Much of traditional Vietnamese ethics was summarized in the Confucian *Ta Hsueh* formula, wherein knowledge and self-cultivation led to proper family regulation, which induced state order, which promoted universal peace."[68]

Prior to colonialism, the villages of Vietnam were self-governed, with a deep-rooted autonomy guaranteed by statutes. According to an old Vietnamese proverb, "the law of the Emperor yields to the custom of the village."[69]

In wars between nations, political objectives are usually sought by destroying the military power of an adversary, but in revolutionary wars, political goals are sought more directly. The focus of conflict is to eliminate the political structure of an opponent and replace it with a political structure of one's own.[70] For the Vietnamese, the revolution was a conflict between *virtue* and *vice*.[71]

During eighty years of rule, France did little that contributed to developing institutions in which the politics of Vietnam could be conducted.[72] Vietnamese political unity disappeared under French rule.[73] To all appearances, Vietnam was governed by an absolute monarch who ruled according to the traditional laws, pomp, and ceremony.[74] He was represented in the provinces by officials appointed by the sovereign.[75] However, in actual fact, the monarchy existed alongside a colonial administration that governed the country under the authority of a resident minister.[76] By 1930 the emperor was no more than a revered idol. Vietnam became "a nation off balance,"[77] and subject to the omnipotence of authoritarian, paternalistic French officials.[78]

While the French administrative structure suppressed a traditional system of politics that had its own unique criteria for mobility and power based on Confucian concepts, it attempted to establish a system with little mobility and almost no power for indigenous participants.[79] At the same time, when social change was occurring more rapidly than ever, no legitimate channels for expressing or reconciling social tension were permitted to a people with a long tradition of lively political life. In destroying the old structures of politics and neglecting to create new ones, France undermined its own interests in Vietnam.[80]

The destabilizing effects of French colonialism had several important consequences in developing the potential for revolution in Vietnam. At the lowest level of the institutional hierarchy, the Vietnamese village was no longer the vital cohesive force it had once been. These qualities were lost to it largely because the French had violated the anonymity of the villagers and the autonomy of the village. This occurred through three major reforms.[81] By weakening traditional village leadership and promoting the legal autonomy of the individual villagers without establishing new forms of political organization to encompass these relationships, the French invited the disintegration of the Vietnamese social system.

John McAlister suggests that perhaps the most important change in creating the potential for revolution in Vietnam was the formation of new sets of elite groups. These elitists emerged from French colonial institutions that were bringing Vietnam into closer contact with the modern world. Besides the administrative cadre, this included people who were naturalized as French citizens, those who received French education, those who became commercial entrepreneurs and property owners, and finally those members of the traditional elite who adapted their talents to qualify for colonial elite status.

McAlister concludes that these changes dislocated the traditional mode of life and produced a poorly integrated society in which a small, urban-oriented, Westernized elite was largely alienated from the bulk of the village-based population. Although harmony was intermittent in traditional Vietnam, it seems to have been a widely shared ideal, especially in the life of the villages. The basis for this harmony was a structure of authority based on Confucian precepts and buttressed by strong patrilineal kinship ties. Since the village is the foundation of Vietnamese society, the deterioration of its resiliency had a strong impact on the stability of the society as a whole.[82]

The Confucian literati who had dominated Vietnam for over a thousand years was swept aside. At the turn of the century, the Vietnamese, who were prominent in the colonial society, were largely Catholic.[83] The changing order was also marked by the decline in learning: the number of traditional schools decreased, the new schools did not make up for the loss, and illiteracy increased.[84] In their classes, Vietnamese children recited: "Our ancestors were called the Gauls."[85] The fear of *mat-muoc* (losing one's country) included concern over the loss not only of sovereignty but even more of identity.[86] The spiritual crisis that resulted from this assault on traditional sources of social cohesion provided the impetus for revolution.

NOTES

1. John T. McAlister Jr., *Vietnam: The Origins of Revolution* (New York: Alfred A. Knopf, 1969), 18.

2. Edwin O. Reischauer and John K. Fairbank, *East Asia: The Great Tradition* (Boston: Houghton Mifflin, 1958), 395.

3. It is important to note that areas neighboring Vietnam in what we now call China were not fully and permanently absorbed into the Chinese central administration (except for the delta province around the city of Canton) until the Trang dynasty (A.D. 618–907) at the earliest, and some parts, such as the Yunnan province, not until the fourteenth century. This uneven pattern of integration emphasizes the changing nature of the Chinese interest in the southern frontier area of which Vietnam was a distant part. For more detail, see Reischauer and Fairbank, *East Asia*, 395.

4. Jean Chesneaux, *The Vietnamese Nation: Contribution to a History* (Sydney: Current Book Distributors, 1966), 68.

5. Confucius held as his aim that "in teaching there should be no class distinctions ... the acceptance of large numbers of students ... without personal questions about them or their families; the giving of equal instruction in each subject, and the teaching of how to read every kind of literary treasure, truly constituted a great step toward emancipation." See Fung Yu-Lan, *A History of Chinese Philosophy: The Period of the Philosophers*, trans. Derk Bodde (Peiping: China Henri Vetch, 1937), 49. Also, Confucius held that "Education begins with poetry, is strengthened through proper conduct and consummated through music." See Lin Yutang, *The Wisdom of Confucius* (New York: Modern Library, 1938), 200.

6. Chesneaux, *Vietnamese Nation*, 68.

7. Ibid., 69.

8. Roger T. Ames, –*Sun-Tzu: The Art of Warfare* (New York: Ballantine Books, 1993), 45.

9. Ibid.

10. Ibid., 46–48.

11. David L. Hall and Roger T. Ames, *Thinking through Confucius* (Albany: State University of New York Press, 1987), 15.

12. Ibid., 12.

13. Ibid., 15.

14. Ames, *Sun-Tzu*, 49–50.

15. Ibid., 41.

16. Hall and Ames, *Thinking through Confucius*, 139.

17. Herrlee Glessner Creel, *Sinism: A Study of the Evolution of the Chinese World-View* (Chicago: Open Court, 1929), 20.

18. Ibid.

19. Hall and Ames, *Thinking through Confucius*, 15.

20. Ibid.

21. Ibid.

22. Ames, *Sun-Tzu*, 50.

23. The epistemological equivalent of the notion of an immanental cosmos is that of conceptual polarity. Such polarity requires that concepts that are significantly related are in fact symmetrically related, each requiring the other for adequate articulation. For a more thorough understanding, see Hall and Ames, *Thinking through Confucius*, 17.

24. Ames, *Sun-Tzu*, 50–52.

25. Creel, *Sinism*, 21–22.

26. Hall and Ames, *Thinking through Confucius*, 135.

27. Ibid.

28. Ibid., 136.

29. Besides the multitude of ordinary spirits, a Heaven (*T'ien*) or God (*Ti*) was supposed to exist, to both of which the *Shu Ching* (Book of History) makes reference in its section, "The Speech of T'ang." See Fung, *A History of Chinese Philosophy*, 30–31. Archaeological evidence consisting of oracle bones and bronze tablets indicate that the people of the Shang dynasty did not conceive of t'ien as a deity. Rather, their religious observances—at least those of the royal house—were centered on *ti*, or *shang-ti*, a concept intimately associated with ancestor worship. *Shang-ti* was cast as an anthropomorphic, personal deity ruling over the human and natural worlds in a manner analogous to the earthly ruler. He could and would intervene in human affairs with regularity and with decisiveness. See Hall and Ames, *Thinking through Confucius*, 202. This doctrine is believed to have originated during the earliest portion of the Chou dynasty—Western Chou, 1122–771 B.C., subsequent to overthrowing the Shang dynasty, as the keynote of the propaganda by which the Chou sought, ultimately with complete success, to reconcile those they had conquered to their rule. See Herrlee G. Creel, *The Origins of Statecraft in China*, vol. 1, *The Western Chou Empire* (Chicago: University of Chicago Press, 1970), 44–45. The family of the Chou kings was believed to be descended from an ancestor called Hou Chi, who became deified. After death the great aristocrats were conceived as living in the heavens, where they supervised the destiny of their posterity. Normally, unless they were extremely displeased with their descendants, they gave them victory in war and prosperity in peace. This established, in theory, the principle that the rulers existed for the sake of the people, rather than the reverse, and that they held their powers only in trust, as a kind of stewardship, subject to revocation if they did not use them well. It would be impossible to exaggerate the importance of this idea for the history of Chinese politics and Chinese thought. See Herrlee G. Creel, *Chinese Thought: From Confucius to Mao Tse-tung* (Chicago: University of Chicago Press, 1953), 11–18. The classical Chinese tradition generally evidences a strong interest in explaining existence by reference to immanental and naturalistic concepts. Such concepts preclude the development of theories that propose to explain the origin and birth of the cosmos per se. *T'ien* is rather a general designation for the phenomenological world as it emerges of its own accord. *T'ien* is wholly immanent, having no existence independent of the calculus of phenomena that constitute it. This can be read as commentary on Mencius' assertion, "He who realizes his natural tendency (*hsing*) realizes t'ien." See Hall and Ames, *Thinking through Confucius*, 206–207.

30. Creel, *The Origins of Statecraft in China*, 82.

31. Ibid.

32. Wm. Theodore de Bary, ed., *Sources of Chinese Tradition* (New York: Columbia University Press, 1960), 8.

33. Ibid.

34. Chinese historians have been fully aware of the various economic and social factors that contribute to the weakening and downfall of one dynasty and the rise of another. Yet they have never, until the most recent times, abandoned the idea that behind these factors and underlying them is a deeper problem of the moral qualification of a man or a family to rule. A ruler may, like the last king of the Shang, be extremely powerful and astute, but if he is selfish and cruel and oppresses his people, Heaven will cease to aid and protect him or sanction his rule, and he will fail. On the other hand a state may be comparatively weak and insignificant, as the early leaders of the Chou are traditionally pictured to have been, but if they are wise and benevolent in their administration and care for their people, then all men will flock to their rule and Heaven will aid them to rise to the highest position. Such is the power and gravity of the heavenly mandate and the moral obligations that it implies. For further detail, see de Bary, ed., *Sources of Chinese Tradition*, 9.

35. Ibid., 8.

36. Creel, *The Origins of Statecraft in China*, 94.

37. See Confucius, *Analects*, 12.7. Also see Yutang, *The Wisdom of Confucius*, 116.

38. See Mencius, 5(1).5.8. Also see David G. Marr, *Vietnamese Anticolonialism, 1885–1925* (Berkeley and Los Angeles: University of California Press, 1971), 103.

39. Creel, *The Origins of Statecraft in China*, 97.

40. Ibid., 441.

41. John T. McAlister Jr. and Paul Mus, *The Vietnamese and Their Revolution* (New York: Harper and Row, 1970), 67.

42. Ibid., 65.

43. Ibid., 65.

44. Ibid., 61.

45. Ibid., 61.

46. Ibid., 61–62.

47. Yutang, *The Wisdom of Confucius*, 198.

48. Creel, *Chinese Thought*, 31.

49. Hall and Ames, *Thinking through Confucius*, 131.

50. Douglas Pike, *History of Vietnamese Communism, 1925–1976* (Stanford, Calif.: Hoover Institution Press, 1978), 11.

51. D.R. SarDesai, *Vietnam: The Struggle for National Unity* (San Francisco: Westview, 1992), 11.

52. Miles Meander Dawson, *The Basic Teachings of Confucius* (New York: New York Home Library, 1942), 172.

53. The family, more than the individual, was the basic unit of Vietnamese society. It embraced the dead as well as the living, tying past generations to those still alive and those yet to come. Each member in death as in life was assured his place in this scheme of things, according to his rank. The family included all those who were directly descended through the male line from the same ancestors. See Ellen Hammer, *Vietnam: Yesterday and Today* (New York: Holt, Rinehart and Winston, 1966), 209.

54. Hue-Tam Ho Tai, *Radicalism and the Origins of the Vietnamese Revolution* (Cambridge: Harvard University Press, 1992), 15.

55. Ibid.

56. Thomas Hodgkin, *Vietnam: The Revolutionary Path* (London: Macmillan, 1981), 23.

57. Ralph Smith, *Viet-Nam and the West* (Ithaca, N.Y.: Cornell University Press, 1968), 14–15.

58. Ibid.

59. "The Great Learning," c. ix., v. 3. See Dawson, *The Basic Teachings of Confucius*, 172.

60. Ibid.

61. Ibid., 173.

62. *Analects*, bk. I., c. ii., v. i.

63. *Analects*, bk. xvii., c. ix., v. 6.

64. *Analects*, bk. ii., c. xxi., v. 2.

65. *Analects*, bk. xxvi., I.

66. Dawson, *The Basic Teachings of Confucius*, 176.

67. Ibid., 178.

68. David G. Marr, *Vietnamese Tradition on Trial, 1920–1945* (Berkeley and Los Angeles: University of California Press, 1981), 103.

69. McAlister and Mus, *The Vietnamese and Their Revolution*, 55.

70. McAlister, *Vietnam*, 4.

71. Hoang Van Chi, *From Colonialism to Communism: A Case History of North Vietnam* (New York: Frederick A. Praeger, 1964), 35.

72. McAlister, *Vietnam*, 13.

73. John DeFrancis, *Colonialism and Language Policy in Viet Nam* (New York: Mouton, 1977), 6.

74. Ibid.

75. Ibid.

76. Ibid.

77. McAlister, *Vietnam*, 49.

78. Jacques Dalloz, *The War in Indo-China 1945–54* (Dublin: Gill and Macmillan, 1987), 8.

79. McAlister, *Vietnam*, 47.

80. Ibid., 47–48.

81. Paul Mus identifies them as: (1) the institution of regular registration of births and deaths, which permitted the composition of more accurate tax rolls; (2) the imposition of tighter French control over the Council of Notables, particularly in tax and budgetary matters; and (3) the substitution of election for co-optation of council members. The first two of these reforms undermined the patriarchal system by curtailing the considerable administrative—and consequently financial—latitude with which the council of notables had been accustomed to function. The third reform encouraged taxpayers to look after their own affairs. For more detail, see Paul Mus, "The Role of the Village in Vietnamese Politics," *Public Affairs* 22 (September 1949), 266.

82. McAlister, *Vietnam*, 49–50.

83. DeFrancis, *Colonialism and Language Policy in Viet Nam*, 155.

84. Ibid.

85. Ibid.

86. Marr, *Vietnamese Anticolonialism*, 95–97.

4

Chun tzu: The Superior (Sage) Man

This chapter details Chinese and Vietnamese traditional elements necessary for the development and identification of the ideal leader's "character." The focus is primarily on Confucian doctrine, followed by Vietnamese adoption and integration of that doctrine into its own culture.

Confucius strove to make the human being good—a good father, a good mother, a good son, a good daughter, a good friend, a good citizen. Confucianism is a system of humanist culture, a fundamental viewpoint concerning the conduct of life and of society. It stood stands for a rationalized social order through the ethical approach, based on personal cultivation. Confucianism attempts to create political order by laying the basis for it in a moral order, and it seeks political harmony by trying to achieve the moral harmony on man himself.[1] For Confucius, man attained personal cultivation when he became a "chun tzu"—a superior man.

Fung Yu-Lan (Fung is the surname) states that in the West, philosophy has been conveniently divided into such divisions as metaphysics, ethics, epistemology, logic, et cetera. And likewise in China we find reference made to the discourse of Confucius on "human nature and the ways of Heaven."[2] In this quotation two of the divisions of Western philosophic thought are mentioned: "human nature" corresponds roughly to ethics, and the "ways of Heaven" to metaphysics. As for the other divisions, such as logic and epistemology, they have been touched on, in China, only by the thinkers of the Period of the Philosophers (extending from Confucius to about 100 B.C.), and have been neglected by later Chinese thinkers (for example, those of the Sung and Ming periods). In one way, to be sure, this later philosophy can be said to have developed a methodology when discussing what is called "the method of conducting study." This method, however, was not primarily for the seeking of knowledge, but rather for self-cultivation; it was not for the search of truth, but for the search of good.

Chinese philosophers for the most part, according to Fung, have not regarded knowledge as something valuable in itself, and so have not sought knowledge for the sake of knowledge; and even in the case of knowledge of a practical sort that might have a direct bearing on human happiness, Chinese philosophers have preferred to apply this knowledge to actual conduct that would lead directly to this happiness, rather than to hold what they considered to be empty discussions about it. For this reason, the Chinese have not regarded the writing of books purely to establish doctrines, as in itself a goal of the highest importance. Most Chinese philosophic schools have taught the way of what is called the "Inner Sage and Outer King." Fung explains that the Inner Sage is a person who has established virtue in himself; the Outer King is one who has accomplished great deeds in the world. The highest ideal for a man is at once to possess the virtue of a Sage and the accomplishment of a ruler, and so become what is called a Sage-king, or what Plato would term the Philosopher-king.

Chinese philosophy, in short, has always stressed what man is (that is, his moral qualities), rather than what he has (that is, his intellectual and material capacities). If a man is a Sage, he remains a Sage even if he is completely lacking in intellectual knowledge; if he is an evil man, he remains evil even though he may have boundless knowledge.[3]

The central idea of Confucianism is that every normal man (refers to every normal human being, to include women and children) cherishes the aspiration to become a superior man—superior to his fellows, if possible, but surely superior to his own past and present self.[4] The theory of imitation, or power of example,[5] results in the doctrine "government by example."[6]

Fung states that, traditionally, Chinese history commences in very early times with the Five Emperors: Fu Shi, Shen Nung or the Divine Farmer, Huang-ti or the Yellow Emperor, Shao Hao, and Chuan Hsu. These semi-divine beings were followed, according to tradition, by Yao, the first really human ruler (supposed to have reigned during the period 2357–2256 B.C.). When Yao died, he was not succeeded by his son, who was considered "unworthy" to receive the empire, but by Shun (2255–2206 B.C.), who had been Yao's minister. During Shun's reign, China was troubled by a terrible flood, and was conquered only after nine years through the heroic efforts of the Great Yu, who constructed dikes and waterways. Yu became emperor after Shun's death and founded the first Chinese dynasty of Hsia. With him, too, the empire became hereditary, the throne passing after his death to his son.

Gradually, however, the Hsia dynasty fell into decay, reaching its lowest depths with its tyrannical last ruler Chieh (1818–1766 B.C.), who is supposed to have engaged in the most abandoned debauches in a park containing, among other things, a lake of wine. A revolt broke out and Chieh was overthrown by a new hero, T'ang, who founded the Shang, also known as the Yin, dynasty (1766–1123 B.C.). This dynasty later also slowly declined, and its last ruler, Chou (1154–1123 B.C.), is said to have rivaled Chieh in cruelty and debauchery.

Meanwhile, the small state of Chou (not to be confused with the name of the ruler Chou) had been gaining power in western China under its ruler King Wen (1184–1157 B.C.). King Wen was succeeded by King Wu (1156–1116 B.C.), who revolted against the tyrant Chou, overcame him, and founded the Chou dynasty (1122–256 B.C.), the longest in Chinese history. After Chou's death, the work of consolidating the empire was greatly furthered by his brother the Duke of Chou, who acted as regent during the early years of the young succeeding king.

Thus, Yao, Shun, T'ang, Kings Wen and Wu, and the Duke of Chou (early Chou is mentioned because there was more than one Duke during this reign) are the sages and heroes par excellence of the Confucians, who always speak of them when referring to the golden age of antiquity.[7] When reference is made to "government by example," good government is represented by identification with Yao, Shun, the Great Yu, King Wen, and King Wu; bad or "evil" government is identified with Chieh and Chou. Yutang states that Confucius believed in history and the appeal of history because he believed in continuity. He offers this reply by Confucius on a question of character regarding "to know the root or foundation of things": What is meant by 'making clear man's character' is this: In the *Announcement to K'ang* (a document in the *Book of History*), it is said, 'He was able to make his character clean.' In *T'aichia* (another document in the same book), it is said, 'He contemplated the *clear* mandates of Heaven.' In the *Canon of Yao* (another document), it is said, 'He was able to make *clear* his great character.' These statements all show that the ancient kings started by making their own characters *clear.*[8]

Confucius describes the *moral ideal* of government:

Guide the people with governmental measures and control or regulate them by the threat of punishment, and the people will try to keep out of jail, but will have no sense of honor or shame. Guide the people by virtue and control or regulate them by *li,* and the people will have a sense of honor and respect.[9]

Thus, character exemplifies government by moral example. "Confucius said, 'A sovereign who governs a nation by virtue is like the North Polar Star, which remains in its place and the other stars revolve around it.'"[10]

Chi K'ang Tzu asked the opinion of Confucius on government, saying, "How would it do to execute the lawless for the good of the law-biding?" "What need, Sir, is there of capital punishment in your administration?" responded Confucius. "If your desire is for good, the people will be good. The moral character of the ruler is the wind; the moral character of those beneath him is the grass. When the grass has the wind upon it, it assuredly bends."[11]

Fung explains that, in other words, in a government through nobility, the mass of the people are uneducated, and hence the ruler's personal conduct inevitably has a great shaping influence on that of the common man. "Confucius said, 'If a ruler rectifies his own conduct, government is an easy matter, and if he does not rectify his own conduct, how can he rectify others?'"[12] The intellectual upper class, at the same time, is a moral upper class, or it fails in its qualifications to be considered the upper class at all. Lin tells us that this is the well-known conception of the Confucian "superior man." This superior man is not at all a super man of the Nietzschean type.[13] He is merely a kind and gentle man of moral principles, at the same time a man who loves learning, who is calm himself and perfectly at ease and is constantly careful of his own conduct, believing that by example he has a great influence over society in general. He is perfectly at ease in his own station of life and has a certain contempt for the mere luxuries of living.[14]

WHAT CONSTITUTES THE SUPERIOR MAN

"In 'The Great Learning,' Confucius says, 'From the highest to the lowest, self-development must be deemed the root of all, by every man. When the root is neglected, it cannot be that what springs from it will be well-ordered.'"[15]

Up to Confucius' time, the term *chun tzu* (gentleman, or superior man) had almost universally had a significance somewhat like the original meaning of our word "gentleman." It denoted a man of good birth, whose ancestors had belonged to a stratum above that of the common herd. Such a person was a gentleman by birth; no one not so born could become a gentleman, and no gentleman could ever become less than one, no matter how vile his conduct might be. Confucius changed this usage completely. He asserted that any man might be a gentleman, if his conduct were noble, unselfish, just, and kind. On the other hand, he asserted that no man could be considered a gentleman merely because he was born one; being a gentleman was solely based on a man's conduct and character.[16]

David Hall and Roger Ames explain that in the Western tradition it is God, or a transcendent realm of forms, or the structure of rationality or the order of nature, that most often constitute the source of guiding values, norms, and principles. Persons or institutions existing within the concrete, historical world may be seen as obedient, in greater or lesser degree, to such principles, but the primary reference of ethical activity is generally to the principle, not the person or institution itself. Exceptions to this generalization are rare. One thinks immediately of Jesus Christ and of Socrates as persons serving as models for Western culture.[17]

Confucius stood for a rationalized social order through the ethical approach, based on personal cultivation.[18] He aimed at a political order by laying the basis for it in a moral order, and sought political harmony by trying to achieve the moral harmony in man himself. Lin states:

Fundamentally, it (Confucianism) originally was a humanist attitude, brushing aside all futile metaphysics and mysticism, interested chiefly in the essential human relationships, and not in the world of spirits or in immortality. The strongest doctrine of this particular type of humanism, which accounts for its great enduring influence, is the doctrine that "the measure of man is man," a doctrine which makes it possible for the common man to begin somewhere as a follower of Confucianism by merely following the highest instincts of his own human nature, and not by looking for perfection in a divine idea.[19]

It is the common man in the street who, having accumulated goodness and wholly completed its cultivation, is called a Sage. First he must seek and then only will he obtain; he must do it, and then only will he reach perfection; he must store it up, and then only will he rise; he must complete its cultivation, and then only can he be a Sage. Thus the Sage is a man who has accumulated (goodness). A man who accumulates (practice in) hoeing and plowing, becomes a farmer; who accumulates (practice in) chopping and shaving wood, becomes an artisan; who accumulates (practice in) trafficking in goods, becomes a merchant; who accumulates (practice in) the rules of proper conduct (*li*) and standards of justice (*I*), becomes a Superior Man.... A man becomes the Superior Man through repeated practice in the "accumulation."[20]

The true manifestations of a man's nature, according to Confucius, need only be blended with good form (*li*) to reach the highest excellence (*jen*), which is hence something that it is possible for all of us to follow and practice.[21] "Therefore *li* is the great weapon or means of power of a sovereign, with which to expose malpractices and beginnings of disorder ... establish the systems of social life ... It is the means by which a country is governed and the sovereign maintains the security of his position."[22] And again with:

The ancients, he said (Confucius), when they wished to exemplify illustrious virtue throughout the empire, first ordered well their states. Desiring to order well their states, they first regulated their families. Wishing to regulate their families, they first cultivated themselves. Wishing to cultivate themselves, they first rectified their purposes. Wishing to rectify their purposes, they first sought to think sincerely. Wishing to think sincerely, they first extended their knowledge as widely as possible.[23]

Fung explains that the Confucian standard for human conduct comes at least partly from within rather than from without; is living rather than dead; and is capable of modification rather than immovable. Therefore, in following the tendencies of our nature, we may differ in our conduct according to time and place. When the genuineness in man's nature expresses itself, it need only be kept in accordance with propriety (*li*) to be of the highest excellence. There is no need to ask whether the human conduct that follows will result in something profitable. As a matter of fact, all human conduct of this kind is either beneficial to society as a whole, or at least can be of no harm. "Be correct in righteousness without considering the profitableness (of the result of the action); be pure in one's principles without considering whether they bring material return.... The Superior Man is informed in what is right (*I*). The inferior man is informed in what is profitable (*li*)."[24]

According to Fung, Confucius says, "In their original natures (*hsing*) men closely resemble each other. In their acquired practices (*hsi*) they grow wide apart."[25]

The aim to excel, if respected by all, approved and accepted by common consent, would appeal to every child and, logically presented to its mind and enforced by universal recognition of its validity, would become a conviction and a scheme for the art of living, of transforming power and compelling vigor.[26] Dawson identifies the Confucian "Art of Living" as:

The practice of right living is deemed the highest, the practice of any other art lower. Complete virtue takes first place; the doing of anything else whatsoever is subordinate.[27] Confucius sets before every man, as what he should strive for, his own improvement, the development of himself—a task without purpose, until he shall "abide in the highest excellence." This goal, albeit unattainable in the absolute, he must ever have before his vision, determined above all things to attain it, relatively, every moment of his life—that is, to "abide in the highest excellence" of which he is at the moment capable. So he says in "The Great Learning": "What one should abide in being known, what should be aimed at is determined; upon this decision, unperturbed resolve is attained; to this succeeds tranquil poise; this affords opportunity for deliberate care; through such deliberation the goal is achieved."[28]

For Confucius, then, the "superior" man becomes a model for society. What, more specifically, is Confucius' understanding of the function of serving as a model? For Confucius, to be is to be in a certain way. A model, therefore, is the actualization of a mode of being.[29] One of the most interesting and dramatic consequences of resorting to models rather than principles in the Confucian tradition is the manner in which it has served to shape the meaning of authority. The primary meaning of authority is discovered in the individual acts of self-actualization associated with creative experience.[30] "Authority" means, ultimately, to be the author of oneself.[31] There is no justifiable sense in which one sought to author or be authored by another.

AFFECTING SOCIOPOLITICAL ORDER

Herrlee Creel asserts that Confucius expected his students to play the dynamic role of revolutionizing any government in which they might take part and making it serve the needs of the people.[32]

The *Chuan* appropriately describes the Superior Man as a leader of men:

The Superior Man, having perfect virtue, is silent, yet his meaning is comprehensible; he does not expand himself, yet is close to others; he does not display anger, yet has an awesome appearance. It is through being cautious in one's own singleness of purpose that one can thus follow in harmony with Fate.

He who would skillfully practice the *Tao*, without sincerity cannot have singleness of purpose (*tu*). Lacking singleness of purpose, he will not gain tangible manifestation. Without such manifestation, although he has ideas and makes them known through his appearance and words, the people may not follow him, or even if they do, will be in doubt.

Heaven and Earth are great, but without sincerity they could not have any effect upon all things. The Sage is intelligent, but without sincerity he could not have any effect upon the people. Father and son are closely related, but without sincerity they would be wide apart. The ruler above is honored, but without sincerity he would be

condemned. Sincerity is what the Superior Man adheres to, and it is the root of government. Where it is, other things of the same kind will come. He who reaches for it will attain it, will become as if light (in weight). Being light, he will move with singleness of
purpose. Moving with unswerving singleness of purpose, he will be complete. Being
complete to the full extent of his ability, ever changing without returning to his original
state, he will be transformed.[33]

Confucius extended the "superior" man's moral qualifications of personal cultivation to political responsibility: "The moral integrity of the ruler, far from
being his private affair, is thought to be a defining characteristic of his leadership.
He must realize that what he does in private is not only symbolically significant
but has a direct bearing on his ability to lead."[34] The cultivation of one's person
necessarily entails active participation both in the family and in the sociopolitical order, not simply in service to others, but as occasions in which to evoke the
compassion and concern that leads to one's own personal growth and refine-
ment.[35] Stated another way, it is inconceivable that full personal growth and disclosure could be achieved in the absence of political responsibility.[36] Confucius
himself states clearly: "To refuse office is to withhold one's contribution of significance (yi).... The superior man's (chun tzu) opportunity to serve in office is
the occasion for him to effect what he judges important and appropriate (yi)."[37]

For Confucius, "a world without order (Tao)" was the result of the breakdown
of the social institutions of his time, and his constant hope was that this condition might be remedied.[38] The Analects contain frequent discussions of "effecting sociopolitical order."

Chi K'ang asked Confucius about effecting sociopolitical order. Confucius replied, "Effecting sociopolitical order means 'ordering.' Where one leads with the example of order, who would dare be otherwise!"[39]

The Master said, "If one is orderly in his own person, what problem would he have in
administering sociopolitical order? But if he is unable to order himself, how can he
bring order to others?"[40]

For this reason, the pursuit of social and political harmony must always begin from personal cultivation.[41]

Fung states that it was Confucius' belief that the degeneration of political and
social states originates from the top. The consequence is that a revolution must
take place among the people. This theory Confucius called the Rectification of
Names (chung ming), a doctrine that he recognized as being of the utmost importance.[42]

Supporting this doctrine, according to Fung, was the belief in *divination* and
magic. The ancient Chinese believed that a close mutual influence existed between things in the physical universe and human affairs. The arts of divination, when arranged, fall into six classes. The third of these classes is connected
with the Five Elements (wu hsing), which are earth, wood, metal, fire, and
water:[43]

The Five Elements are the corporeal essences of the Five Constant Virtues.[44] The *Shu* (Book of History) says: "The first category is called the Five Elements. The second is called reverent practice of the five functions.[45] This means that the five functions should be used in consonance with the Five Elements. If one's personal appearance, speech, vision, hearing and thought lose their proper order, the Five Elements will fall into confusion and changes will arise in the five planets. For these all proceed from the numbers connected with the almanac, and are divisions of one thing (i.e., of the movements of the Five Elements). Their laws all arise from the revolutions of the Five Powers[46] (i.e., Elements), and if they are extended to their farthest stretch, there is nothing (in the universe) which they will not do.[47]

When Confucius spoke of Heaven, he meant a ruling or personal Heaven. The *Chuang-tzu*, for example, speaking of the movements of Heaven, Earth, sun, and moon, says, "Is there perhaps a mechanical arrangement that makes these bodies move inevitably the way they do? Is it perhaps that they keep revolving without being able to stop themselves?"[48] Fung says that this is clearly a naturalistic cosmology, and so is Hsun Tzu's: "Heaven has a constant regularity of activity. It did not exist for the sake of Yao nor cease to exist for the sake of Chieh. Respond to it with good government, and success will result. Respond to it with misgovernment, and calamity will result."[49]

For Confucius neither person nor society is subordinated as an instrumental means to serve the realization of the other; rather, they stand as mutually implicatory ends. Any and all semblance of order in society and the state is ultimately traceable to and is an integral feature of the personal ordering of its constituents.[50] Confucius on numerous occasions moves to underscore the interdependence of sociopolitical order and the ordering of the particular person.

Tzu-lu asked about becoming a superior person (*chun tzu*).

> The Master said, "In cultivating himself he inspires reverence."
>
> "Is that all there is to it?" Tzu-lu asked.
>
> "In cultivating himself he brings peace and stability to others."
>
> "Is that all there is to it?"
>
> "In cultivating himself he brings peace and security to the common people. Even Yao and Shun were not able to accomplish this."[51]

Confucius, given his distinctly social perspective with regard to the project of person-making, does not perceive a corresponding degree of difference between private and public interests, between ethical and political concerns, between social and political structures.[52] There are important consequences of the fact that in Confucian social theory a person is irreducibly communal, especially when weighed against the concerns of our own tradition.

Mencius expounds on this social theory regarding the Superior Man: "If there were no men of a superior grade (*chun tzu*), there would be no one to rule the countrymen. If there were no countrymen, there would be no one to support the men of superior grade."[53] Fung reinforces Mencius with: "State and society are like a great tree or a gem. To rule them one must belong to the class of specialists who 'spend their youth in studying.' It is the men of great virtue and worth who comprise this class of specialists capable of governing the state and society." According to this principle, says Fung, governmental office is the highest of all positions, and must be filled by persons of the greatest virtue.[54]

Creel aptly summarizes the relation of man and ethical conduct in government.

Confucius' object[ive] was good government, and this he believed to be possible only when the government was administered by men who, in addition to being educated in the ordinary sense, were also endowed with integrity and poise. "What," he asked, "has one who is not able to govern himself to do with governing others?" He believed, in fact, that heads of state and all officers of the government should provide an example of the highest type of conduct, and he believed that by doing so they could accomplish more than by any amount of either preaching or punishment.[55]

The *Ta Hsueh* says that

the Superior Man requires from others only the qualities that he himself has, and blames others only for the qualities that he himself lacks. Never has there been a man who could teach others without having reference to what is stored up in his own person. Therefore the government of the state depends upon the regulation of the family.... When the ruler as a father, a son, an elder or a younger brother, is a model, then the people imitate him. The fact that if the ruler acts as a model, his people will model themselves upon him, means that cultivation of the person becomes the foundation for regulating the home, ruling the state, and bringing peace to the world.[56]

The *Chung Yung* says:

The universal Way for all under Heaven is five-fold, and the (virtues) by means of which it is practised are three. There are the relations of ruler and subject, father and son, husband and wife, elder and younger brother, and of friend and friend; these five constitute the universal Way for all. Wisdom (*chih*), human-heartedness (*jen*),[57] and fortitude (*yung*): these three are universal virtues for all. That whereby they are practised is one. Some are born and know it; some study and so know it; some through painful difficulties come to know it. But the result of their knowing is all one. Some naturally practise it; some easily practise it; some do so by dint of strong effort. But the result accomplished comes to one and the same thing.

The Master said: "To be fond of learning is to be near to wisdom; to practise (virtue) with vigor is to be near to human-heartedness; to know to be ashamed (of one's errors) is to be near to fortitude. He who knows these three things knows how to cultivate his own person. Knowing how to cultivate his own person, he knows how to govern others. Knowing how to govern others, he knows how to govern the empire and state."[58]

In summary, Creel aptly asserts Confucius' steadfast emphasis on the qualitative rather than the quantitative aspects of the superior man: "The measure of man's life is not 'how long?' but 'how good?'."[59]

THE VIETNAMESE SUPERIOR MAN

In the idealized Vietnamese world, teachers and students were bound as strongly and enduringly as fathers and sons. As the saying went, *nhut phu nhi su* (first comes the father then comes the teacher). This idea was vividly illustrated on New Year's Day when a student, after extending greetings to his father, immediately went to his teacher's home to do likewise before paying respect to his mother. In Tonkin, where the Confucian ethos was far stronger than in Cochinchina, the same word—*thay*—applied to both father and teacher, emphasizing their overlapping duties in promoting the material and moral welfare of the young men in their care. Just as fathers performed their tutorial duties, so did teachers act as surrogate fathers.[60] Together they taught the accumulated wisdom and values of past generations. In return, they expected lifelong respect and obedience.[61]

Alexander Woodside states that the avowed goal of traditional education was to turn a scholar into a superior man (*quan tu;* Chinese *chun tzu*) through self-cultivation.[62] But self-perfection was only a first step toward political office. The motto of the superior man was: "Cultivate thyself, set thy house in order, govern thy country, pacify All-Under-Heaven."[63] Underlying this motto was the assumption that individual self-cultivation led naturally to family management and then to political rule. An official was regarded as the *dan chi phu mau* (father and mother of the people). It was his responsibility to look out for their welfare and, like any father, he expected to be obeyed and respected by them. Teachers, therefore, were supposed to prepare their students not only for the examinations but also for their future role as "fathers and mothers of the people." Vietnamese officials clung to this self-image long after French administrators, having usurped the mandarins' power, assumed the rhetorical role of fathers of the immature and wayward Vietnamese population.

In summary, we see how Confucian doctrine influenced the development of "character." This character was cultivated more from the act of "doing" than from the act of "saying," or discourse, which the rhetor used to create his own image. Also, character development was an ongoing process that took a lifetime to achieve. Very few individuals throughout Chinese and Vietnamese history were honored with the title chun tzu.

NOTES

1. Lin Yutang, *The Wisdom of Confucius* (New York: Modern Library, 1938), 6.
2. *Lun Yu,* V 12. See Fung Yu-Lan, *A History of Chinese Philosophy: The Period of the Philosophers,* trans. Derk Bodde (Peiping: China Henri Vetch, 1937), 1.
3. Fung, *A History of Chinese Philosophy,* 2.
4. Miles Meander Dawson, *The Basic Teachings of Confucius* (New York: New York Home Library, 1942), 1.

5. Confucius also believed in history and the appeal of history because he believed in continuity. He regarded *character, position of authority,* and the *appeal to history* as the three essential requisites for governing, and that lacking any one of these things, no one could succeed with a governmental system and "command credence," however excellent it might be. See Yutang, *The Wisdom of Confucius,* 32.

6. Ibid., 22–23.

7. Fung, *A History of Chinese Philosophy,* xv–xvi.

8. Yutang, *The Wisdom of Confucius,* 141.

9. Ibid., 198.

10. Ibid., 199.

11. Fung, *A History of Chinese Philosophy,* 60–61.

12. Yutang, *The Wisdom of Confucius,* 199–200.

13. Ibid., 23.

14. Ibid.

15. Dawson, *The Basic Teachings of Confucius,* 7.

16. Herrlee G. Creel, *Chinese Thought from Confucius to Mao Tse-tung* (Chicago: Chicago University Press, 1953), 27.

17. David L. Hall and Roger T. Ames, *Thinking through Confucius* (Albany: State University of New York Press, 1987), 177.

18. Yutang, *The Wisdom of Confucius,* 6.

19. Ibid.

20. Fung, *A History of Chinese Philosophy,* 288.

21. Ibid., 78.

22. Yutang, *The Wisdom of Confucius,* 233.

23. Dawson, *The Basic Teachings of Confucius,* 8–9.

24. Fung, *A History of Chinese Philosophy,* 75.

25. Ibid., 75

26. Dawson, *The Basic Teachings of Confucius,* 2.

27. Li Ki, bk. xvii., sect. iii., 5. See Dawson, *The Basic Teachings of Confucius,* 6.

28. Dawson, *The Basic Teachings of Confucius,* 6–7.

29. Hall and Ames, *Thinking through Confucius,* 180.

30. Ibid.

31. Ibid.

32. Creel, *Confucius: The Man and the Myth,* 76.

33. Fung, *A History of Chinese Philosophy,* 293.

34. Tu Wei-ming, *Centrality and Commonality: An Essay on Chung-Yung* (Honolulu: University of Hawaii Press, 1976), 71.

35. Hall and Ames, *Thinking through Confucius,* 184.

36. Ibid.

37. See *Analects* 18:7.

38. Fung, *A History of Chinese Philosophy,* 59.

39. See *Analects* 12:17.

40. See *Analects* 13:13.

41. See *Analects* 13:6.

42. Fung, *A History of Chinese Philosophy,*. 293–294.

43. Ibid., 294.

44. *Wu ch'ang*. These are the Confucian virtues of benevolence, righteousness, propriety in demeanor, wisdom, and good faith (*jen, I, li, chih,* and *hsin*).

45. The five functions are personal appearance, speech, vision, hearing, and thought.

46. These powers (*Te*)—that is, the Five Elements—are earth, wood, metal, fire, and water. Each one is supposed to overcome the preceding, and in its turn be overcome by the next, in endless succession. Each of which is supposed to preside over one period in history. See Fung, *A History of Chinese Philosophy,* n.1, 160.

47. Ibid., 27.

48. Ibid., 284–285.

49. Ibid., 285.

50. Hall and Ames, *Thinking through Confucius,* 160.

51. See *Analects* 14:42.

52. Hall and Ames, *Thinking through Confucius,* 160.

53. Fung, *A History of Chinese Philosophy,* 114.

54. Ibid., 114.

55. Herrlee G. Creel, *Confucius: The Man and the Myth* (New York: John Day, 1949), 76.

56. Fung, *A History of Chinese Philosophy,* 365.

57. Confucius said that "the man bent on public service, if he be the human-hearted kind of man, under no circumstances will he seek to live at the expense of his human-heartedness." See *Chinese Philosophy in Classical Times* (New York: E.P. Dutton, 1944), 20.

58. Fung, *A History of Chinese Philosophy,* 373.

59. Creel, *Confucius: The Man and the Myth,* 133.

60. Much of traditional Vietnamese ethics was summarized in the Confucian *Ta Hsueh* formula, wherein knowledge and self-cultivation led to proper family regulation, which induced state order, which promoted universal peace. See David Marr, *Vietnamese Tradition on Trial, 1920–1945* (Berkeley and Los Angeles: University of California Press, 1981), 103.

61. Alexander B. Woodside, *Community and Revolution in Modern Vietnam* (Boston: Houghton Mifflin, 1976), 97.

62. Ibid., 97.

63. "Tu than, te gia, tri quoc, binh tien ha"; Chinese: "hsiu shen, chi chia, chih kuo, p'ing t'ien-hsia."

5

Ho Chi Minh: The Chun tzu

The ancients used to like to sing about natural beauty:
Snow and flowers, moon and wind, mists, mountains
and rivers.
Today we should make poems including iron and steel,
And poets also should know how to lead an attack.[1]

In this chapter, I identify and explicate the primary elements of Ho Chi Minh's reconstitutive rhetoric. These include the substantive themes and arguments of his discourse, his second persona (discourse), and his first, or personal, persona. Within the first persona are detailed accounts of his character, writings, speeches, and poems.

Ho's rhetorical prowess for the audiences that comprised the independence movement in French colonial Indochina was clearly the *sin qua non* of his career. That prowess is as puzzling as it is undeniable. Ho's persuasion parallels the lingering inability to understand the nationalist movements and their appeal in Far East Asia in the period between the two world wars. Ho's rhetoric exemplifies how Vietnamese nationalism and cultural heritage invited and can be effectively embodied in the rhetor's substantive themes and arguments, second persona, and first or personal persona. Based on this analysis, I suggest that when these rhetorical components, combined with cultural heritage, are reciprocal and complementary as in the case of Ho Chi Minh, they comprise a rhetorical formula[2] that helps to explain his persuasion. In their most potent form the rhetorical components seem to coalesce in a merger of the rhetor's thought and character that can reconstitute individuals into audiences capable of carrying out nationalist policies.

SUBSTANTIVE THEMES AND ARGUMENTS OF HO CHI MINH'S DISCOURSE

Freedom

We have sometimes been weak, and sometimes powerful, but at no time have we lacked heroes.

—*Proclamation of Emperor Le Loi* in 1418, at the start of a ten-year war
of independence against the Chinese

One becomes a revolutionary because one is oppressed. The more oppressed one is, the more unshakably resolved one is to carry out the revolution.[3]

—Ho Chi Minh

Ho Chi Minh's speeches, essays, and interviews contain two broad and pervasive themes. The first rested the nationalist case on principles reminiscent of
Thomas Jefferson and the founding fathers of the United States, and the French
Revolution of 1791. Convinced of the existence and importance of enduring values and timeless truths, Ho incessantly instructed his audience on the importance of freedom or the right for self-determination. For example, in 1919, Ho
presented, to the Versailles Peace Conference, an eight-point petition demanding basic freedoms for the Vietnamese:

1. General amnesty for all Vietnamese political prisoners.
2. Equal rights for Vietnamese and French in Indochina, suppression of the Crimi-
    nal Commissions which are instruments of terrorism aimed at Vietnamese patri-
    ots.
3. Freedom of press and opinion.
4. Freedom of association and assembly.
5. Freedom to travel at home and abroad.
6. Freedom to study and the opening of technical and professional schools for na-
    tives of the colonies.
7. Substitute rule of law for government by decree.
8. Appointment of a Vietnamese delegation alongside that of the French govern-
    ment to settle questions relating to Vietnamese interests.

Although Ho's voice was not heard by President Woodrow Wilson, his efforts
did not go entirely unnoticed.[4] A Vietnamese student of the time, Bui Lam, set
down his somewhat idealistic impressions of the period in *Souvenirs sur Ho Chi
Minh* (Recollections of Ho Chi Minh):

At Versailles, where the imperialists were sharing the colonial cake, a Vietnamese called
Nguyen Ai Quoc had made an unheralded demand for self-determination in Vietnam.
To us, it was like a flash of lightning, the first thunderclap of spring.... Here was a Viet-
namese insisting that his people be accorded their rights. We took our hats off to him.
No two Vietnamese residing in France could meet, after this, without mentioning the
name Nguyen Ai Quoc.[5]

Although brief, this attempt resonated among the Vietnamese in France and especially in Vietnam. Thus began Ho's long and tireless quest for Vietnamese independence.

By August 1922 the French government ordered the French secret police to follow Ho's movement throughout Paris. "An Open Letter To M. Albert Sarraut, Minister Of Colonies," printed in *Le Paria*, 1 August 1922, was a response to this action:

Your Excellency, we know very well that your affection for the natives of the colonies in general, and the Annamese in particular, is great.... As a Chinese poem says, "The wind of kindness follows the movement of your fan, and the rain of virtue precedes the tracks of your carriage." As you are now the supreme head of all the colonies, your special care for the Indochinese has but increased with your elevation.

You have created in Paris itself a service having the special task—with special regard to Indochina, according to a colonial publication—of keeping watch on the natives, especially the Annamese, living in France.... But "keeping watch" alone seemed to Your Excellency's fatherly solicitude insufficient, and you wanted to do better. That is why for some time now, you have granted each Annamese—dear Annamese, as Your Excellency says—private-*aides-de-camp*. Though still novices in the art of Sherlock Holmes, these good people are very devoted and particularly sympathetic. We have only praise to bestow on them and compliments to pay their boss, Your Excellency. In consequence, while remaining obliged to you, we respectfully decline this distinction flattering to us but too expensive to the country. If Your Excellency insists on knowing what we do every day, nothing is easier: We shall publish every morning a bulletin of our movements, and Your Excellency will have but the trouble of reading.

Besides, our timetable is quite simple and almost unchanging.
Morning: from 8 to 12 at the workshop.
Afternoon: in newspaper offices (leftist, of course) or at the library.
Evening: at home or attending educational talks.
Sundays and holidays: visiting museums or other places of interest.
There you are! Hoping that this convenient and rational method will give satisfaction to Your Excellency, we beg to remain ...
Nguyen Ai Quoc[6]

The Fifth Congress of the Communist International was held in Moscow from 17 June to 8 July 1924. Ho used this opportunity to condemn colonialism and expose lost freedoms.[7] In the "Report on the National and Colonial Questions at the Fifth Congress of the Communist International," Ho wrote:

What have the bourgeois class in the colonialist countries done toward oppressing so many people enslaved by them. They have done everything.... I shall begin with my country.... French colonial policy has abolished the right of collective ownership and replaced it by private ownership.... It has also abolished small ownership to the advantage of big ownership of the plantations.... In all the French colonies, famine is on the increase and so is the people's hatred. The native peasants are ripe for insurrection.

The year 1926 was an important one for Ho. It was at this time he demonstrably altered his discourse from denouncing "freedom lost" to "revolution" and "revolutionary parties" in his quest for a free Vietnam. In Thanh Nien[8] he wrote:

What is the primary requisite for revolution? First, it is necessary to have a revolutionary party which, internally, can motivate and organize the masses and which, externally, can contact oppressed peoples and the proletarian class everywhere. A strong revolutionary party is a prerequisite to success just [as] a strong helmsman is a strong prerequisite to the operation of a boat.[9]

The essence of Thanh Nien's teaching was contained in *Duong Cach Menh* (Revolutionary Path), the very important work Ho wrote early in 1926. The "ABC of revolution," was used as a training manual for Thanh Nien cadres. Ho Chi Minh began with a section, which even preceded the introduction, dealing with "the behavior of a revolutionary":

> Personally a revolutionary must be thrifty,
> show himself friendly but impartial,
> be resolute to correct his errors ...
> be greedy for learning,
> be persevering,
> adopt the habit of studying and observing,
> place the national interests above personal interests,
> be neither conceited nor arrogant ...
> be little desirous of material things,
> know how to keep secrets.
> Dealing with others he must
> be generous towards each,
> be serious-minded toward the Party,
> be always ready to give guidance,
> be straightforward without being rough,
> know how to judge other people.

The qualities defined here mark a whole generation of the first revolutionary militants. Note the style and syntax, in principle, it mirrors Confucian descriptions of the *chun tzu* and is written in classical Chinese form.

The central purpose of *Duong Cach Menh* was to provide a revolutionary theory that would

"make everyone understand why he must make the revolution; why it is impossible not to make it; and why it must be done immediately, not with one person sitting around waiting for another person to do it." Because the making of the revolution is an urgent task, "Yes, we say everything here in a simple, quick and firm way, like two times two make four, without any painting or decoration.... We have to shout loudly, work fast, in order to save our race. How can we find time to polish the writing?"[10]

Duong Cach Menh represented a turning point in the history of the Vietnamese patriotic and revolutionary movement, marking a break with the past and the assertion of new principles and ideas.[11]

On 3 February 1930, Ho made an appeal at the Internationale conference to found the Vietnamese Communist Party;[12] his petition was unanimously approved. His prophetic appeal was for all Vietnamese to join this new party:

Preparations are being actively made to launch a second imperialist war. When this war breaks out, the French imperialists will surely drive our brothers and sisters into a criminal slaughter.... The French imperialists' inhumane oppression and exploitation have helped our people realize that with revolution we will survive and without revolution we will die ... the Vietnamese Communists who had not previously been organized, are now united into a party—the Viet-Nam Communist Party—to lead all our oppressed brothers and sisters to revolution.

As of now, we must join the Party, we must help it and follow it in order to carry out the following mottoes: Overthrow the French imperialists; fight for the total independence of Indochina; establish a government of workers, farmers, and soldiers; confiscate the banks, the plantations, and other enterprises of the imperialists and place them under control of the government of workers, farmers, and soldiers; implement an 8 hour day, abolish government obligations, poll tax, and give exemptions to the poor; bring the rights of freedom to the people; implement education for the masses; and implement equality between the sexes.

By 1930, Ho Chi Minh had become a champion of the Vietnamese peasant. In a report made to the Communist Internationale in July 1939, Ho wrote:

The Party ... should only claim for democratic rights, freedom of organization, freedom of assembly, freedom of press and freedom of speech, general amnesty for all political detainees, and struggle for the legalization of the Party.... The Party cannot demand that the Front recognizes its leadership. It must instead show itself as the organ which makes the greatest sacrifices, the most active and loyal organ.[13]

In "Letter From Abroad (1941)"[14] we see the call for revolution:

Since the French were defeated by the Germans, their forces have been completely disintegrated. However, with regard to our people, they continue to plunder us pitilessly, suck all our blood, and carry out a barbarous policy of all-out terrorism and massacre. Concerning their foreign policy, they bow their heads and kneel down, shamelessly cutting our land for Siam; without a single word of protest, they heartlessly offer our interests to Japan. As a result, our people suffer under a double yoke: they serve not only as buffaloes and horses to the French invaders but also as slaves to the Japanese plunderers.... Living in such painful and lamentable conditions, can our people bind their own hands and doom themselves to death? No! Certainly not! ... Now, the opportunity has come for our liberation....

Compatriots throughout the country! Rise up quickly! Let us follow the heroic example of the Chinese people! ... Some hundreds of years ago, when our country was endangered by the Mongolian invasion, our elders under the Tran dynasty rose up indignantly and called on their sons and daughters throughout the country to rise as one in order to kill the enemy. Finally they saved the people from danger, and their good name will be carried into posterity for all time.... Let us unite together! As one in mind and strength we shall overthrow the Japanese and French and their jackals in order to save people from the situation between boiling water and burning heat. I pledge to use all my modest abilities to follow you, and am ready for the last sacrifice.... Victory to Viet-Nam's Revolution!

On 16 August 1945, Ho hastily convened a conference to approve a general order for insurrection.[15] Ho wrote in the "Appeal for General Insurrection:

Because unity is strength, only strength enables us to win back independence and freedom.... At present, the Japanese army is crushed.... In the Front our compatriots
march side by side without discrimination as to age, sex, religion, or fortune.... The decisive hour in the destiny of our people has struck. Let us stand up with all our strength
to free ourselves! ... Forward! Forward! Under the banner of the Viet Minh Front,
move forward courageously![16]

The document is signed, for the last time, "Nguyen Ai Quoc."[17]

On 2 September 1945, in Hanoi at Ba Dinh Square, addressing a crowd of approximately one hundred thousand people, Ho Chi Minh declared the independence of the Democratic Republic of Vietnam. He spoke in the name of the Viet
Nam Doc Lap Dong Minh Hoi (League for the Independence of Vietnam), or
the Vietminh.[18] In declaring independence, Ho stated:

After the Japanese had surrendered to the Allies, our whole people rose to regain our
national sovereignty and to found the Democratic Republic of Viet-Nam. The truth is
that we have wrested our independence from the Japanese and not from the French....
Emperor Bao Dai has abdicated. Our people have broken the chains which for nearly a
century have fettered them and have won independence for the Fatherland. Our people
at the same time have overthrown the monarchic regime that has reigned supreme for
dozens of centuries. In its place has been established the present Democratic Government.... For these reasons, we, members of the Provisional Government of the Democratic Republic of Viet-Nam, solemnly declare to the world that Viet-Nam has the right
to be a free and independent country—and in fact it is so already.

Throughout his address, Ho chose to stress the theme of freedom rather than
equality,[19] which had come to symbolize class conflict and national disunity.[20]
But it was collective, not individual freedom he talked about, as his closing words
made clear: "Vietnam has the right to enjoy freedom and independence, and in
fact, has become a free and independent nation. The whole Vietnamese people
is resolved to bring all its spirit and its power, its life, and its possessions to preserve this right to freedom and independence."[21]

Equality

Ho Chi Minh's second theme was that of equality or the right not to be bru-
tally exploited. In an important address delivered in France, on Christmas Day
1920, in the Loire Valley town of Tours, at the Eighteenth National Congress of
the Socialist Party,[22] Ho pleaded for adherence to the Third International for one
single reason: the colonial question. Relentlessly, and to the obvious discomfort
of the mainland French delegates, Ho ticked off one French crime in Indochina
after another:

In its selfish interest [France] conquered our country with bayonets. Since then we have
not only been oppressed and exploited shamelessly, but also tortured and poisoned pitilessly. Plainly speaking, we have been poisoned with opium, alcohol,[23] etc.... Prisons
outnumber schools.... Any natives having socialist ideas are arrested and sometimes

murdered without trial.... We have neither freedom of press nor freedom of speech. Even freedom of assembly and freedom of association do not exis.... We are forced to live in utter ignorance and obscurity because we have no right to study.... Thousands of Vietnamese have been led to a slow death or massacred to protect other people's interests.... And they are said to be under French protection! I cannot, in some minutes, reveal all the atrocities that the predatory capitalists have inflicted on Indochina.[24]

Ho ended his appeal with a passionate plea that the "Socialist Party must act practically to support the oppressed natives."[25]

In "Le Proces de la Colonisation Francaise," a treatise of some thirty thousand words, Ho began with an examination of French overseas recruitment for World War I, which had then (1917) reached a peak of slaughter that France was on the brink of exhaustion. Desperate to widen her conscription net, she had reached out into her colonies. The recruitment of the natives had been called "voluntary," but Ho was at pains to demonstrate that this word, when applied to subject peoples, had an elastic interpretation. Each French district commissioner directed the mandarins of his area to round up so many "recruits" within a certain time by whatever methods he deemed necessary. Only those Vietnamese able to pay adequate ransom could escape what was, in effect, conscription. Relatives of conscripts who happened *dulce et decorum* to give their lives for the motherland were rewarded with licenses to sell opium. Ho wrote, "Thus the colonial government committed two crimes against humanity. Not satisfied to promote the vice of opium, they tied it to the victims of fratricide butchery and rated life so cheaply that they thought this putrid recompense quite sufficient for the death of a loved one."[26]

Ho also cited, with savage irony, the occasion of a commission charged to organize a fete to collect funds toward a "Monument to Dead Annamites." Ho:

There was to be a fair, a country dance and a garden party. The attractions were to be numerous and variegated and would include the attendance "not only of aviators but all the elite for miles around." A buffet of magnificent splendor would offer satisfaction to the most exacting gourmet. We shall certainly show the dead Annamites that we know how to appreciate their sacrifice.[27]

Ho's attack was delivered as if by an armchair anarchist. In denouncing the inequities, he was fairly wise if not always wisely fair. He endeavored to prove his accusations with facts. He knew something about history, about economics, about the political structure of the world, and about human nature; and he knew that if you wish to sound reveille you must blow your bugle shrilly.

There is nothing theoretical about Ho's writings in *Le Paria* and other journals of the period. He understood that Vietnam's case as a colonial country was not exceptional but rather was typical of the whole colonial system. In his early writings, he showed a constant concern for other colonial struggles in Africa, the Middle East, and Latin America. Bernard Fall states, "His early writings clearly reflect the personal humiliations he must have suffered at the hands of the colonial master—not because they hated him as a person, but simply because, as a 'colored' colonial, he *did not count* as a *human being.*"[28] This intense personalization of the whole anticolonial struggle shined clearly throughout Ho's writings. He was not interested in debating general political theories. He was far more interested in demonstrating that particular (fully named) French colonial officials were sadists who enjoyed harassing their colonial charges. He would rather write about this than patiently whittle away at the colonial structure in the hope that it would, in its own time and on its own conditions, yield a small measure of self-government to the subject nation.

In "Some Considerations on the Colonial Question,"[29] printed in *L'Humanite*, 25 May 1922, Ho revealed the general ignorance of the French people concerning the vast populations within the French colonies. He also illuminated the prevailing indifference of the French government as to their welfare, an indifference that was broken only by periods of ferocious reprisals when the slaves made protests.[30] In an excerpt subtitled "Fierceness of Repression," Ho wrote:

If the French colonialists are unskillful in developing colonial resources, they are masters in the art of savage repression and the manufacture of loyalty made to measure. The Gandhis and the De Valeras would have long since entered heaven had they been born in one of the French colonies. Surrounded by all the refinements of courts martial and special courts, a native militant cannot educate his oppressed and ignorant brothers without the risk of falling into the clutches of his civilizers.[31]

Ho wrote many articles that attacked the iniquities of colonialism beyond the confines of the French empire. An example of this was printed in *La Vie Ouviere*. This awareness of the conflict on an international scale reflected his gradual absorption of Leninism. The articles in *Le Paria* range widely, but a good proportion were scarifying indictments of French colonial exploitation and brutality or bitterly ironic "open" letters to key colonial figures or hierarchic fringe. When, for example, the Emperor Khai Dinh of Annam visited France in 1922 and was made a great fuss of, Ho's open letter ridiculed this hypocrisy: "Apart from the racehorses at Longchamps and the pretty Frenchwomen at the Opera, what else has Your Majesty deigned to see in the course of Your instructive visit to the poetical land of France?" (Thereby nicely anticipating the behavior of the subsequent Annamese emperor, the better-known Bao Dai.) It was also with a view to satirizing this "imperial dynasty" that Ho wrote a playlet entitled *The Bamboo Dragon*, apparently his one and only venture in this field.[32]

"Racial Hatred," printed in *Le Paria*, 1 July 1922, identified some of the injustices inflicted upon Vietnamese natives that had gone unpunished by the colonial government:

For having spoken of the class struggle and equality among men, and on the charge of having preached racial hatred, our comrade Louzon[33] has been sentenced. Let us see how the love between peoples has been understood and applied in Indochina of late.

We will not speak for the time being of the poisoning and degradation of the masses by alcohol and opium of which the colonial government is guilty; our comrades in the parliamentary group will have to deal with this matter one day.... A certain Pourcignon furiously rushed upon an Annamese who was so curious and bold as to look at this European's house for a few seconds. He beat him and finally shot him down with a bullet in the head. A railway official beat a Tonkinese village mayor with a cane. M. Beck broke his driver's skull with a blow from his fist. M. Bres, building contractor, kicked an Annamese to death after binding his arms and letting him be bitten by his dog. M. Deffis, receiver, killed his Annamese servant with a powerful kick in the kidneys.... Has justice punished these individuals, these civilizers? Some have been acquitted and others were not troubled by the law at all. That's that.... And now, accused Louzon, it's your turn to speak![34]

As a final example of Ho's almost savage bitterness at this time, he wrote in "Annamese Women and French Domination," printed in *Le Paria*, 1 August 1922:

Colonization is in itself an act of violence of the stronger against the weaker. This violence becomes still more odious when it is exercised upon women and children.... Colonial sadism is unbelievably widespread and cruel.... . On the arrival of the soldiers, relates a colonial, the population fled; there only remained two old men and two women: one maiden, and a mother suckling her baby and holding an eight-year-old girl by the hand. The soldiers asked for money, spirits, and opium.

As they could not make themselves understood, they became furious and knocked down one of the old men with their rifle butts. Later, two of them, already drunk when they arrived, amused themselves for many hours by roasting the other old man at a wood fire. Meanwhile, the others raped the two women and the eight-year-old-girl. Then, weary, they murdered the girl. The mother was then able to escape with her infant and, from a hundred yards off, hidden in a bush, she saw her companion tortured. She did not know why the murder was perpetrated, but she saw the young girl lying on her back, bound and gagged, and one of the men, many times, slowly thrust his bayonet into her stomach and, very slowly, draw it out again. Then he cut off the dead girl's finger to take a ring, and her head to steal a necklace.[35]

Consistent with Ho's attacks on individual administrative officials, he wrote in "An Open Letter To M. Albert Sarraut, Minister of Colonies," printed in *Le Paria*, 1 August 1922:

Your Excellency,

We know very well that your affection for the natives of the colonies in general, and the Annamese in particular, is great.

Under your proconsulate the Annamese people have known true prosperity and real happiness, the happiness of seeing their country dotted all over with an increasing number of spirit and opium shops which, together with firing squads, prisons, "democracy," and all the improved apparatus of modern civilization, are combining to make the Annamese the most advanced of the Asians and the happiest of mortals.

These acts of benevolence saves us the trouble of recalling all the others, such as enforced recruitment and loans, bloody repressions, the dethronement and exile of kings, profanation of sacred places, etc.

As a Chinese poem says, "The wind of kindness follows the movement of your fan, and the rain of virtue precedes the tracks of your carriage."

These attacks continued with "An Open Letter To M. Leon Archimbaud," printed in *Le Paria*, 15 January 1923, which was meant to inform the public of French colonial atrocities covered up in Vietnam.

You state that if France has sinned in colonial matters it is rather from an excess of generous sentiment than anything else. Will you tell us, M. Archimbaud, whether it is out of these generous sentiments that the natives are deprived of all rights to write, speak, and travel, etc.? Is it out of these same sentiments that the ignoble condition of "native" is imposed on them, that they are robbed of their land only to see it given to the conquerors, and forced thereafter to work as slaves? Is it also from an excess of generosity that you are doing all you can to intoxicate the Annamese with your alcohol and stupefy them with your opium? ... While you are waiting to receive "one of the finest claims to glory that can be dreamt of," allow me to tell you, M. Archimbaud, that if Victor Hugo had known that you would write such stuff today in his newspaper, he would never have founded it.[36]

In "An Appeal from the Peasant International to the Working Peasants in the Colonies,"[37] the audience moved from the French citizen to that of the oppressed citizenry in the colonies; however, the message remained the same. Ho wrote:

Peasants in the colonies, modern slaves who, in millions, in the fields, savannas, and forests in the two continents, are suffering under the double yoke of foreign capitalism and your local masters.... Even more than your peasant brothers in the metropolitan countries, you put up with long working hour[s], poverty, and insecurity.... You are compelled to do forced labor, backbreaking poterage, and endless corvees.... You pay crushing taxes....

Not content with thus reducing you to poverty and ruin, capitalism is dragging you from your homes and your fields, to turn you into cannon fodder and throw you, in fratricidal wars, against other natives or against the peasants and workers of the metropolitan country.... Join your action to ours; let us struggle together for our common emancipation!"

In 1923, the Soviet poet Osip Mandel'stam met Ho Chi Minh. An account by Mandel'stam of the meeting and his impressions of Ho and the Vietnamese people was published in the *Plamya*,[38] on 23 December 1923.

"Then what effect did the Ghandi movement have upon Indochina? Was there any echo, any repercussion over there at all?" I asked Nguyen Ai Quoc.

"No," the man with whom I was talking replied. "Our Vietnamese people, peasants, are living in a long dark night—with no press, no information whatsoever about what is happening in the world; night, it is really night...."

Nguyen Ai Quoc mentioned the word "civilization" with disgust. He had travelled to nearly every colony in the world, to North Africa and Central Africa, and he had seen enough. In our talk, he repeatedly mentioned the word "brothers." Brothers here meant black people, Indians, Syrians, Chinese....

"At 13 years of age, for the first time I heard the French words: liberty, equality and fraternity. To us, all white men were French. Thus I wanted to get acquainted with French civilization, to learn what lay behind those words. But in local schools, the French taught us as if we were parrots. We were kept uninformed, and we were not allowed to read newspapers and books. Not only were we prevented from reading new authors, but even Rousseau and Montequieu we were not allowed to read as well.... We Vietnamese are just slaves. Not only are we not permitted to go abroad, we cannot even travel within the country.... People are bought with money.... The French are poisoning our people. They have set up a coercive 'alcohol' drinking system. Who can drink their kind of alcohol! Too much alcohol has been made, too much. So, the Governor General ordered a per-capita distribution of alcohol to the people, forcing the people to buy and drink a kind of alcohol nobody wants."

By the end of 1923, Ho had become well known in Europe—as well as in the colonies—China, North Africa, and his homeland of Vietnam. His continued assault on colonialism was tireless. "Annamese Peasant Condition," printed in *La Vie Ouvriere*, 4 January 1924, was a scathing account of the French intervention:

The Annamese in general are crushed by the blessings of French protection. The Annamese peasants especially are still more odiously crushed by this protection: as Annamese they are oppressed: as peasants they are robbed, plundered, expropriated, and ruined. It is they who do all the hard labor, all the *corvees*. It is they who produce for the whole horde of parasites, loungers, civilizers, and others. And it is they who live in poverty while their executioners live in plenty and who die of starvation when their crops fail. This is due to the fact that they are robbed on all sides and in all ways by the Administration, by modern feudalism, and by the Church ...

From this brief survey, one can see that behind a mask of democracy, French imperialism has transplanted in Annam the whole cursed medieval regime, including the salt tax, and that the Annamese peasant is crucified on the bayonet of capitalist civilization and on the Cross of prostituted Christianity.[39]

In a historic interview of Ho Chi Minh by Italian correspondent Giovanni Gernacetto entitled "Talk with a Vietnamese Student on the Soviet Revolution and the Soviet Oriental Institute," printed in L'Unita, 15 March 1924, Ho pointed out the secret of success in the revolutionary undertaking to liberate his country, which was to follow the Soviet revolutionary path. He concluded the interview saying, "The people who come to civilize our country do not want us to enjoy freedom. Nevertheless, we will continue to follow the path laid by the October Revolution. We will put into practice all the lessons we have learned."[40]

Ho's relentless attack on the effects of colonial policy offer a broader perspective in "Indochina and the Pacific," printed in *La Correspondance Internationale* 18 (1924):

According to an official avowal, the colonies in the Pacific are afflicted with debility, and are living—if we can call it living—at a slower and slower rate. The truth is that populous islands are being entirely depopulated, in a short time, by alcohol and forced labor....

Most islands in the French Pacific have been yielded to concessionary companies which rob the natives of their land and make them work as slaves....

It is not enough to demoralize the whole Annamese race with alcohol and opium. It is not enough to take 40,000 "volunteers" yearly for the glory of militarism. It is not enough to have turned a people of 20 million souls into one big sponge to be squeezed by money-grubbers. We are, on top of all this, to be endowed with slavery....

Since the Washington Conference,[41] colonial rivalries have become sharper and sharper, imperialist follies greater and greater, and political conflicts more and more unavoidable. Wars have been launched over India, Africa, and Morocco. Other wars may break out over the Pacific area if the proletariat is not watchful.

Early in 1925, Ho, in cooperation with M.N. Roy, established the short-lived Hoi Dan Toc Bi Ap Buc The Gioi (League of Oppressed Asian Peoples), a broad front of Koreans, Indonesians, Malaysians, Indians, and Chinese, as well as Vietnamese.[42] One of the organization's most important functions—perhaps *the* most important function—was the production of the journal *Thanh Nien*. About one hundred copies of each issue were produced by lithographic stone, which were then taken clandestinely and distributed in Bac Bo, Trung Bo, Nam Bo, Laos, and even Thailand. The range of the journal's influence was far wider than its circulation, since it was read by all Thanh Nien members, in the country and outside it, as well as by a large body of supporters who copied and recopied it many times. It had a longer life than *Le Paria* and, like *Le Paria*, survived the withdrawal of its creator and principal editor and contributor Ho Chi Minh. The first issue of *Thanh Nien* appeared on 21 July 1925, and it continued on a weekly basis until the eighty-eighth issue, in April 1927, when Chiang Kai-shek carried out his counterrevolutionary coup and massacre of Kwangtung Communists and Ho escaped to Moscow.[43]

"Lenin and the East," printed in *Le Siffet* (Paris), 21 January 1926, elevated Lenin, and at the same time, condemned the West for its injustices toward his people.

On the orders of these gentlemen, native villages were bombed and colonial peoples suppressed in a ruthless and cruel manner that no words can depict. Everybody knows that the opportunists have carried out a policy of segregating the white workers from the colored workers, that the trade unions, under the influence of these wily socialists, do not want to admit workers of different color into their ranks. The colonial policy of the Second International has more than anything else laid bare the true face of this petit-bourgeois organization. Hence, until the October Revolution, socialist theories were regarded as theories particularly reserved for the Whites, a new tool for deceit and exploitation. Lenin opened a new era, which is truly revolutionary, in various colonies.

"French Colonization on Trial," written during the latter part of 1930, was a scathing attack on French militarism—the conscription of colonized natives who either fought in World War I or were placed in colonial service:

Before 1914, they were only dirty Negroes and Dirty Annamese, at the best only good for pulling rickshaws and receiving blows from our administrators. With the declaration of the joyful new war, they became the "dear children" and "brave friends" of our paternal and tender administrators and of our governors—more or less general. They [the natives] were all at once promoted to the supreme rank of "defenders of law and liberty." This sudden honor cost them rather dear, however, for in order to defend that law and that liberty of which they themselves are deprived, they had suddenly to leave their rice fields or their sheep, their children and their wives, in order to cross oceans and go and rot on the battlefields of Europe.

On 2 September 1945, in Hanoi, at Ba Dinh Square, the first sentence of Ho's declaration of independence addressed the issue of equality.[44]

All men are created equal; they are endowed by their Creator with certain unalienable Rights; among these are Life, Liberty, and the pursuit of Happiness.

This immortal statement was made in the Declaration of Independence of the United States of America in 1776. In a broader sense, this means: All the peoples on the earth are equal from birth, all the peoples have a right to live, to be happy and free.

The Declaration of the French Revolution made in 1791 on the Rights of Man and the Citizen also states: "All men are born free and with equal rights, and must always remain free and have equal rights."

Those are undeniable truths.

Nevertheless, for more than eighty years, the French imperialists, abusing the standard of Liberty, Equality, Fraternity, have violated our Fatherland and oppressed our fellow citizens. They have acted contrary to the ideals of humanity and justice.

As we have seen, Ho Chi Minh's themes (ideology) of freedom and equality were basic yet powerful. These themes defined inherent motives and interests that a rhetoric can appeal to. To be reconstituted as a Vietnamese peasant in the terms of Ho's narratives was to be reconstituted such that freedom, independence, and equality were not only possible but necessary. Without freedom and independence, this reconstitutive rhetoric would have ultimately died and those it had reconstituted would have ceased to be subjects, or at least would have remained, within their current circumstance. In consequence, true Vietnamese nationalists could not have ignored Ho's pleas for active participation in the liberation of their country. Only by participation would they have been in harmony with their being and their collective destiny: "Inhumane oppression and exploitation have helped our people realize that with revolution we will survive and without revolution we will die."[45]

In sum, Ho Chi Minh's discourse called on those he had addressed to follow narrative consistency and the motives through which they were reconstituted as audience members.

SECOND PERSONA AND THE EXPECTATION OF A LEADER

Frederick Antczak combines ideas drawn from Plato, Kenneth Burke, and Wayne Booth to explain how a rhetorical merger of thought and character affords an identification with an audience in a way that allows its members to discover and activate latent qualities in themselves. Antczak takes the concept from Plato that a rhetoric that can intellectually and morally reconstitute audiences rather than merely indulge them must make use of the character of both audience and speaker; and from Burke, that the center of the rhetorical enterprise is identification, a consubstantiality achieved between rhetor and auditor through sharing of substance.[46] Booth supplies the ideas that "the primary mental act of man is to assent ... 'to take in' and 'even to be taken in'" through rhetorical exchanges, and that "by understanding and being understood, by taking in other selves, we expand our moral and intellectual capacities, we expand our identities ourselves."[47] Thus, for Burke and Booth, "intellectual reconstitution inextricably involves human character."[48] Applying his model to the discourse of Ralph Waldo Emerson, Mark Twain, and Henry Adams, Antczak demonstrates how such rhetoric can reformulate audiences, liberating listeners to think and act more creatively, intelligently, and humanely.[49]

Edwin Black describes the second persona as the implied auditor, "a model of what the rhetor would have his real auditor become."[50] John Hammerback adds one important element to this: "the rhetor's rhetorical creation in audiences of an expectation for a leader who possesses particular qualities which are identified by the rhetor."[51] To Hammerback's definition I will add one more important element: the rhetor's rhetorical creation in audiences of an expectation for a leader who possesses particular qualities that are identified, not by the rhetor, but rather by cultural heritage.

The Vietnamese expectation for a leader required more than discourse, it required fulfillment of a 4,500-year-old legacy: the "Mandate from Heaven" and the "concept of revolution." In his insightful explication of the nature, processes, and effects of such discourse, as referred to by Hammerback, Maurice Charland illuminates the rhetorical power of the second persona within the context of the text, the framework of ideology, and the material world inhabited and impacted by human agents.[52] In so doing, he draws broadly from the thought of Black, Burke, Michael McGee, and writers on narrative, structuralism, hermeneutics, and various related topics.[53]

In the Rhetoric of Motives, Kenneth Burke proposes "identification" as an alternative to "persuasion" as the key term of the rhetorical process. Burke's project is a rewriting of rhetorical theory that considers rhetoric and motives in formal terms, as consequences of the nature of language and its enactment. Burke's stress on identification permits a rethinking of judgment and the working of the rhetorical effect, for he does not posit a transcendent subject as audience member, who would exist prior to and apart from the speech to be judged, but considers audience members to participate in the very discourse by which they would be "persuaded." Audiences would embody a discourse. A consequence of this theoretical move is that it permits an understanding within rhetorical theory of ideological discourse, of the discourse that presents itself as always only pointing to the given, the natural, the already agreed upon.[54]

Ho wrote of Lenin after his death. "Lenin and the Peoples of the East," printed in *Le Paria*, 27 July 1924, showed how Ho attempted to make the nexus for identification between the "ideal auditor" of the East and that of Communism. Ho spoke of Lenin, "It is not only his genius, but his disdain of luxury, his love of labor, the purity of his private life, his simplicity, in a word, it is the grandeur and beauty of this master which exert an enormous influence upon the Asian peoples and irresistibly draw their hearts toward him." [55]

We see one of the first examples of the "ideal auditor" in Ho's "Appeal in Connection with the Founding of the Indochinese Communist Party," February 1930, in which he stated: "Workers, Farmers, Soldiers, Youths, Students! Oppressed and Exploited Compatriots! The Indochinese Communist Party has been founded. It is the Party of the workers' class." In claiming a "Party of the workers' class," Ho eliminated, for the first time, class status and created a new identification for the masses. To this he added, "It [the Party] will guide the proletariat into the leadership of the revolution." It is important to note that Ho claimed the "leadership" will guide the new party and not "Ho Chi Minh" will guide the new party, or "Ho Chi Minh and the new Party" will guide the "workers' class."[56] Unlike Western discourse, in which the individual rises above the party and proclaims his or her vision for the people, Ho offered leadership through the collective efforts of the "Party." This is a subtle yet important strategy for Ho. He remained faithful to the tradition of the collectivity while presenting a totally new political ideology—a polar opposite to Confucianism—to the people. This is a permanent theme throughout Ho's discourse. In "The Line of the Party during the Period of the Democratic Front," printed in *Tuyen Tap* (Selected Works), in July 1939, Ho stated, "The party cannot demand that the front recognize its right of leadership, but the party must demonstrate that it is the most sacrificial, most active, and most loyal element."[57]

In a "Letter from Abroad" (1941), Ho called for a singular people, dismissing class lines, "As one in mind and strength we shall overthrow the Japanese and French.... He who has money will contribute his money, he who has strength will contribute his strength, he who has talent will contribute his talent. I pledge to use all my modest abilities to follow you, and am ready for the last sacrifice." Ho called for each individual to contribute according to their ability, as would be expected in the collective, to make the revolution successful, as one would make the village successful. He substituted "revolution" (and with it implied the "Party") for village.

Appeals to Cultural Heritage

From a "Talk with a Vietnamese Student on the Soviet Revolution and the Soviet Oriental Institute," printed in *L'Unita*, 15 March 1924, Ho appealed to cultural heritage when describing qualities of Vietnamese leadership: "My comrades have placed all confidence and zeal in their tasks. We clearly understand that we are assuming very heavy responsibilities, and that the future of the colonial peoples depends on our propaganda and self-sacrificing spirit."

In 1927, Chiang attacked the Chinese Communists and massacred many of them. Ho was still busy teaching in Whampoa. The course had to be stopped at once and the students were obliged to return home as best they could. A few days later, Ho met a group of them at Canton, and making use of an old Chinese proverb, sought to hearten them by saying: "Don't be discouraged by the recent setback. Remember that a storm is a good opportunity for the *Tung* (pine) and the *Ba* (cypress) to show their strength and their stability."[58]

In a "Letter from Abroad" (1941), Ho appealed to history and heritage in an effort to move the masses to join the liberation movement:

Compatriots throughout the country! Rise up quickly! Let us follow the heroic example of the Chinese people! ... Some hundreds of years ago, when our country was endangered by the Mongolian invasion, our elders under the Tran dynasty rose up indignantly and called on their sons and daughters throughout the country to rise as one in order to kill the enemy. Finally they saved their people from danger, and their good name will be carried into posterity for all time. The elders and prominent personalities of our country should follow the example set by our forefathers in the glorious task of national salvation.... Rich people, soldiers, workers, peasants, intellectuals, employees, traders, youth, and women who warmly love your country! ... Let us unite together!

Ho cited the Tran dynasty[59] as a historical appeal, for all Vietnamese were familiar with its history. He concluded with, "The sacred call of the Fatherland is resounding in your ears; the blood of our heroic predecessors who sacrificed their lives is stirring in your hearts! ... Unite with each other, unify your action to overthrow the Japanese and French."

In his appeal after the national resistance against the French began, Ho Chi Minh said: "The strength of the enemy is like fire. Our strength is like water. Water will overcome fire."[60] This is a reference to the Five Elements from traditional Chinese philosophy, in which one element overcomes the other according to its strength.

To enter into Ho Chi Minh's rhetorical narrative is to "identify with Black's second persona ... to exist at the nodal point of a series of identifications and to be captured in its structure and in its production of meaning ... to be a subject which exists beyond one's body and life span ... to live towards national independence."[61] Ho's discourse describing the colonial conditions in Vietnam created that series of identifications, which, over time, captured the hearts and minds of the peasantry. The power of Ho's discourse and personal persona is the power of an embodied ideology. This form of an ideological rhetoric is effective because it is within the bodies of those it constitutes as subjects.[62]

To what extent did the Vietnamese people identify with Ho's second persona? At the time, anticolonial literature was banned in Vietnam: newspapers, fliers, books, and booklets were confiscated by the colonial administration, yet the peasantry regularly received Ho's appeals which were printed in European newspapers.[63] "A bamboo stick on which was engraved an appeal had been secretly sent from one village to another. It had been sent from one place to another—and thus a collusion had been made. The Vietnamese had to pay a high price for such an action. Hundreds of them had been executed because of such actions."[64]

FIRST PERSONA

> Everything evolves, it is the cycle of nature:
> After the rainy days, the fine weather comes,
> In an instant, the whole world shakes off its damp clothes,
> Thousands of li of mountains unfurl their brocade carpet.
> Under the warm sun and the clean wind, the flowers smile,
> In the big trees with branches washed clean, the birds make chorus.
> Warmth fills the heart of man and life reawakens.
> Bitterness now makes way for happiness.
> This is how nature wills it.[65]

Ho's absence had not robbed him of any relevance or political position; over the years he had added steadily to his reputation.[66]

Early in the nineteenth century, the Frenchman Chaigneau, who had spent the greater part of his adult life serving the Emperor Gia-Long and held the post of a senior mandarin at the court of Hue, said about the Vietnamese: "Do not expect invention from them, but be assured that their talent for imitation will never be at fault."[67]

Through his own rhetorical efforts and his steadfastness to the Confucian belief of the *chun tzu*, Ho Chi Minh himself displayed the characteristics he had encased in his profiles of the model auditor and of the nationalist-Communist leader. The sources of his identification were his heritage; his physical appearance and much of his own life's experiences, partially providential, but primarily a result of his calculated design; the content and style of his discourse; and most important, the consciously crafted self-portrait he presented throughout his life.

Ho's style of speech and writing touched the Vietnamese deeply; his speeches were vivid and simple.[68] Bui Lam, a compatriot of Ho's, recalls:

After the Russian revolution, Lenin not only identified his objectives with downtrodden people everywhere, he offered help. This was why [I] felt tied to the Soviet Union and grew bolder. Soon [I] was reading *Le Paria*, where articles signed Nguyen Ai Quoc "roused me as if a fire were burning in my head." I dashed out to find some of my fellow countrymen and we read to each other. Tears came to our eyes. How could the short and concise articles so much rouse up the heart and soul of those who had lost their country, of the oppressed and exploited toilers? They urged us to action! But we were at a loss as to what was to be done. It came to our minds that we had to see Nguyen Ai Quoc.[69]

Additional excerpts from *Plamya* 23 December 1923, regarding Mandel'stam and his impressions of Ho and the Vietnamese people reveal some of Ho's qualities:

Nguyen Ai Quoc was the only Vietnamese in Moscow, representing the old Malayan race. Wearing a knitted jacket, he looked like a boy, small, thin and quick. He talked in French, the language of his people's oppressors, but the French words uttered from his mouth sounded so sober and unpolished as if they were the repressed sounds of his native language.

"I was born into a Confucian scholar family... Confucianism is not a religion, but rather a philosophy of ethics and proper conduct. Basically, Confucianism also preaches 'harmony in the society.'"

The whole face of Nguyen Ai Quoc generated his inherent decency and sophistication.... From the person of Nguyen Ai Quoc generated a whole culture, not the European culture, but perhaps the culture of the future.

Unlike his contemporary, Mao Tse-tung, whose writings sometimes had a philosophical vein, Ho was always most concerned with the specific problems of people.[70] He did not limit his written attacks to colonialism, he also wrote of injustices committed against blacks in the United States. In "Lynching," printed in *La Correspondence Internationale* (1924), Ho wrote,

It is well known that the black race is the most oppressed and most exploited of the human family.... What everyone does not perhaps know, is that after sixty-five years of so-called emancipation, American Negroes still endure atrocious moral and material sufferings, of which the most cruel and horrible is the custom of lynching.... In a wave of hatred and bestiality, the lynchers drag the Black to a wood of a public place. They tie him to a tree, pour kerosene over him.... While waiting for the fire to be kindled, they smash his teeth, one by one. Then they gouge out his eyes. Little tufts of crinkly hair are torn from his head, carrying away with them bits of skin, baring a bloody skull.... The Black can no longer shout: his tongue has been swollen by a red hot iron. His whole body ripples, trembling, like a half-crushed snake. A slash with a knife: one of his ears falls to the ground.... And the ladies tear at his face.... "Popular justice," as they say over there, has been done.

In Canton, sometime in 1925, Ho taught a short (two-to-three-month) "Special Political Course for the Vietnamese Revolution," as it was called on a plate affixed to the classroom door.[71] Le Hong Phong, a former student of Ho's, recalls:

He [Ho] used to stop at difficult words and to give long explanations until everybody could understand. He urged his students to engage in free discussions, to ask questions, and then answered all the problems raised. He took part in the debates organized by the study groups and asked the brightest students to help the weaker ones. He checked the notes taken by each one and gave them advice. According to Comrade Nguyen Luong Bang he even took the trouble to give a course of general education.... He taught English to Nguyen Luong Bang.

Through the conversations held between teacher and students, "we realized," said Le Manh Trinh, "with great astonishment that, even though he had left the country a long time ago, Vuong [Ho Chi Minh] was thoroughly up-to-date with what was going on at home."[72]

In the cave at Pac Bo, in 1941, Ho instructed his comrades—who naturally saw things only from the narrow angle of their local situation—and gave them the benefit of his worldwide experience.[73] He translated Sun Tsu's *Art of War-*

fare[74] and wrote the pamphlet entitled "Guerrilla Warfare: Experiences of the Chinese Guerrillas."[75]

Maintaining Confucius' position on education, Ho wrote in *Prison Diary*, "The civilized and the uncivilized must struggle by nature; the majority through education, will win.... For a usefulness of 10 years, cultivate a tree; for a usefulness of 100 years, cultivate a man."[76]

A few years later, in September of 1945, Ho wrote a "Letter to Graduating Students," stating:

whether the rivers and mountains of Vietnam are beautiful, and whether Vietnam becomes an equal power with the other nations of the world depends mainly on the learning of the children. Therefore, the working man must study to raise his level of education.... To build socialism, we must increase production; to increase production, we must have advanced techniques; to use advanced techniques, we must have education."[77]

Character

In addition to his remarkable intelligence, Ho was endowed with an outstanding personality. In fact, he had all of the qualities necessary to be a leader, and his austerity, perseverance, iron determination, and wholehearted devotion to the cause of the revolution were an inspiration to all who served under him and to the nation as a whole.[78] Hoang Van Chi says of Ho:

Ho became ... a living idol amongst his people. Not only was his photograph placed on every family altar, but in a few places ... people even bowed before his image as they set out to work in the rice fields. Ho lives the life of an aesthetic, never indulging in any comfort that is not strictly necessary.... For years he dressed as a peasant, wearing a Canadian windcheater and a pair of sandals made from a discarded tire. His whole appearance was an assurance that he had devoted his life to the service of the people. Having renounced his family early in life and being unmarried, Ho stands above all suspicion of nepotism and corruption, and would thus seem above the reach of calumny."[79]

To quote Paul Mus,

He is an intransigent and incorruptible revolutionary in the manner of Saint-Just.... Thus, by his moral standing alone, Ho acquired the respect and confidence of the whole Vietnamese nation. His reputation for honesty and sincerity has contributed greatly to his success, for in Vietnam, as in many underdeveloped countries, the masses put their trust in the personal character and behavior of a leader more than in the political party he represents.[80]

Unlike Mao and his colleagues, Ho never carried a rifle with him. His only weapons were his tongue, his pen, his native wit, his strong moral fiber, his passionate devotion to the cause of his people, and his determination to achieve his set purpose against all odds.[81] Ho was not a military leader like Tito or the Burmese Patriotic Socialists, nor a party boss like Rakosi or Kim Il Sung; rather, he was first and foremost a man of the people, liking people of all sorts and all walks of life, trusting people until he found them to be false, ready to condone their political heresies if they were prepared to work loyally with him for the common cause, and willing to listen to what they had to say rather than to lecture to them on party doctrine and discipline.[82] For Ho, works were more important than faith, devotion more valuable than discipline.[83]

Ho Chi Minh was a man of immense warmth, charm, and understanding, one who cared passionately for his fellow countrymen. Through all the long years of struggle, from his early revolutionary days as he traveled the countryside to his ultimate occupancy of the Presidential Palace, the man himself remained unchanged.[84]

William Warby adds:

Ho had always considered himself a "soldier sent to the front by the people." In him, love for the people became a fierce passion.... Food, comfort and clothing were of no great consequence to Ho. His concern was for his people, and he had unswerving faith in them.... During the years before Ho returned to Hanoi, he kept himself busy, even in his rare free time, studying, gathering firewood or visiting old people and children. He organized training courses for them and taught the children to read and write.... The Vietnamese loved and respected Ho Chi Minh because for over a half century he had struggled tirelessly to save his country. His spirit was that of a man who was not seduced by riches, shaken by poverty nor corrupted by power.... President Ho Chi Minh and Uncle Ho were one and the same man.[85]

David Halberstam describes Ho as one of the extraordinary figures of this era—part Gandhi, part Lenin, all Vietnamese. He says of Ho that he was, perhaps more than any single man of the century:

the living embodiment to his own people—and to the world—of their revolution. He was an old Bolshevik and a founding member of the French Communist party (what could be more alien to the average Vietnamese peasant?); yet to most Vietnamese peasants he was the symbol of their existence, their hopes, their struggles, their sacrifices and their victories. (Even after Dienbienphu, when many people of North Vietnam became angry with the Communist regime, they were always careful to exclude Ho from their blame: the Communists were responsible for the bad things—Ho, Uncle Ho, for the good things.) To the population he was always the symbol they needed: he was the gentle Vietnamese, humble, soft-spoken, mocking his own position, always seen in the simplest garb, his dress making him barely distinguishable from the poorest peasant—a style that Westerners for many years mocked, laughing at the lack of trappings of power, of uniform, of style, until one day they woke up and realized that this very simplicity, this cult of simplicity, this capacity to walk simply among his own people was basic to his success."[86]

In contrast, Graham Greene wrote in 1956 about Ngo Dinh Diem, the American-sponsored leader in the South: "He is separated from the people by cardinals and police cars with wailing sirens and foreign advisers droning of global strategy when he should be walking in the rice fields unprotected, learning the hard way how to be loved and obeyed—the two cannot be separated."[87]

Time magazine in 1948 referred to Ho contemptuously as "goat-bearded," a "Mongoloid Trotsky," and a "tubercular agitator who learned his trade in Moscow."[88] Halberstam states that it was:

that very same contempt—which every peasant in Vietnam felt from every Westerner—that would make him so effective. This was Ho's great strength, the fact that he was a Vietnamese Everyman, and it was why he shunned monuments and marshals' uniforms and generals' stars, for he had dealt with powerful Westerners all his life, had surely been offered countless bribes by them, but he had chosen not to be like them, not to dress like them or live like them. Rather, he remained a Vietnamese, a peasant, a man like one's ancestors—pure, uncorrupted in a corrupting world, a man of the land and its simplest virtues.[89]

Halberstam continues his description of Ho stating that in a country where the population had seen leaders reach a certain plateau and then become more Western and less Vietnamese, corrupted by Western power and money and ways, and where, the moment they had risen far enough to do anything for their own people, immediately sold out to the foreigners, the simplicity of Ho was powerful stuff. The higher he rose, the simpler and purer Ho seemed, always retaining the eternal Vietnamese values: respect for old people, disdain for money, and affection for children.[90]

Ho deliberately did not seek the trappings of power and authority, as if he were so sure of himself and his relationship to both his people and history that he did not need statues and bridges, books and photographs to prove it to him or them.[91] One sensed in him such a remarkable confidence about who he was, what he had done, that there would be no problem communicating it to his people; indeed, to try to communicate it by any artificial means might have created doubts among them. His abstinence from his own cult was particularly remarkable in the underdeveloped world, where the jump from poor peasant to ruler of a nation in a brief span of time often proves very heady stuff and inspires more than the predictable quota of self-commemoration.[92]

There is something else in Ho's character that one does not find in any other top political figure, not even (to mention two considered more humane) Gandhi and Nehru. This is what Confucius called *shu*.[93] There is no exact equivalent in English; the nearest we might get is "reciprocity" in the sense of those responses between two human beings aware of the concept that all men are brothers. Ho's instinct seemed to have been to work from the heart rather than from the head.[94] "To see something, to feel something and then interpret one's impressions; to try and distinguish between the appearance and reality of things; that's all. What's so difficult about it?"[95]

Ho was always intimate, always accessible, always truly "uncle." Compare this to the remoteness and austerity of Mao or even Chou.[96] Ho could say that he hated the French and mean it, but this was a hatred of what certain Frenchmen had done to his family, his friends, or his countrymen. Charles Fenn states that there is seldom, if ever, an instance when he translated this impersonal animosity into specific hatred of one individual. A person whom Ho had reason to hate—Louis Arnoux, chief of the Indo-China Secret Police, who opposed Ho and even hounded him for twenty years—was able to speak of him with liking and respect—a feeling that could scarcely have been inspired by any hate on Ho's part.[97]

Jean Sainteny claims that Ho's enemies never doubted the genuineness of his manners: "How could he have held the pose for such a long time and so perfectly if it were not authentic?" adds Sainteny. "We should remind ourselves that he and all the ministers of his government lived very simply. Although they entertained in the former French palaces, they lived very modestly in cramped quarters or in small villas. Their vow of poverty was never violated."[98]

A man becomes wise at sixty—such is the rule of the Confucian order under which Ho Chi Minh began his life.[99] Ho therefore became wise when the war against the French was at its height. "But he was also wise enough to avoid any cult of his own personality even after the victory when his position in North Vietnam was practically unchallenged," asserts Reinhold Neumann-Hoditz. To this he adds, "In Ho's lifetime there was no personality cult of the kind which has surrounded Mao Tse-tung." His picture was rarely displayed on public buildings. And the theoretical party journal *Hoc Tap* was able to note on one of the president's birthdays that Uncle Ho was loved and respected but not revered as a god.[100]

Ho's title of *Bac* must be understood in the context of Chinese culture in which the eldest members of society (Ho himself refers to them repeatedly in his appeals) enjoy especial veneration. *Bac* means "big uncle"; it is the term used to denote the elder brother of a father or mother while the younger brother is referred to as *Chu* (little uncle).[101] It was only natural that people began to speak of Bac Ho because his closest colleagues already belonged to a younger generation. *Bac* is, therefore, a familiar term, and the Communists in North Vietnam like to point out that every family considered Bac Ho an honored member. In addition, *Bac* is synonymous with democratic conduct: the father can command, but the uncle only advises. The relations were unique between this leader of a Communist Party and state and his people from whom he demanded the most severe deprivations.[102]

Robert Shaplen writes that Ho was the beaming father figure of his people, the man of constant simplicity, the soft-spoken Asian who seemed gentle, indeed almost sweet, sometimes self-mocking. His humor and warmth were in sharp contrast to the normal bureaucratic grimness of a high Communist official.[103]

Shaplen also praises Ho when he writes that in her long history Paris had taken to heart innumerable celebrities, "but perhaps there has never been one who achieved more spontaneous popularity. Upon his arrival he was still only a name in the newspaper; upon leaving he was almost as much Uncle Ho in France as in Vietnam." Shaplen describes the scene:

Ho enjoyed a huge success, he charmed everyone. He was widely compared to Confucius, to the Buddha, to St. John the Baptist. Everywhere he went, whether to the opera, to a fancy reception, to a picnic or to a press conference, he appeared in his simple, high-buttoned linen work suit. His wit, his oriental courtesy, his *savoir-faire*, his mixed profundity and playfulness in social intercourse, his open love for children, above all his sincerity and simplicity, captured one and all.[104]

And finally, Mus tells us that Ho cited the four virtues he considered as pre-eminent to be: diligence, frugality, justice, and integrity.[105]

Personal Testimonies

Hoang Quang Binh, a revolutionary agent whose hairdresser's shop served as a meeting place for the railway workers, recalled three visits by Ho. The first visit included Phung Chi Kien in early 1940.[106]

Ho and Kien stayed to give talks to the railway workers and to start a training course for the Party cell members. The lectures given by Uncle Ho were very concise. Explaining dialectical materialism, he quoted actual facts from the workers' situation. He used simple words such as those of a story teller and always ended his speech by asking whether and how well we understood him. Uncle would get up very early. Though the house was narrow and the attic rickety, he still did physical training. Then he cleaned out the room. A poor, dark and untidy attic thus became more orderly, better aired and even seemed better lit.

During the day, while I was busy cutting hair, he split firewood and boiled rice, while Kien prepared vegetables. Even my wife, who had grown perverse from a life of hard-bargaining, was very pleased because Uncle helped her fetch and carry. He looked after my son Hai even better than I did, putting him to bed, covering him several times during the night, keeping him warm against pneumonia, bathing and washing him many times and teaching him to be clean.[107]

Ho got them all to come along to the stream and bathe. Ho was always fond of cleanliness. The first time I cut his hair he told me "You had better wash this apron often and you will get more customers. All work must be well done. The more so, since our shop only caters for workers." [There was another hairdresser in the town who catered for "clerks," train masters, and employees working in the French quarter.] He was always very thrifty. He only smoked cigarettes he rolled himself, although ready-made cigarettes saved a lot of bother. Whenever I had money to spare I would buy some for him.

At Xi Xuyen there was a very cruel station master who had a girl of about thirteen as a servant. He used to beat her most savagely. Infuriated, we wanted to give him a thrashing. Meanwhile, Uncle asked the girl about her native place and her parents, and we learned that she was an orphan sold by an uncle of hers to this train master. Non-plused for a while, then sighing, Uncle said to us, "Beating the cruel man would not remove the cause of the evil. That is why we have to wage a revolution."[108]

The following is from the second visit.

On this occasion Ho stayed with Hoang about a month. It was to be four years before they met again. Meanwhile, Ho had spent eighteen months in Chinese prisons. One afternoon in late 1944, I was doing a haircut when I saw a thin, tired-looking old man stepping into my shop. Realizing to my surprise that he was Tran [an alias used by Ho], I wanted to leave the customers who were waiting; but he told me to continue. He was dressed like a Chiang Kai-shek soldier with a cap covering his big forehead, a jacket patched with many pieces, and worn-out grass shoes bespattered with mud.... Seeing that Uncle was so tired, I inquired about his health. "I am weary and even ill," he said... ..Although feverish with malaria, Ho had only a single threadbare blanket. (This is one of the very few occasions when Ho reveals the hardships of his travels.)[109]

Hoang concluded his reminiscences with an account of his third meeting.

It was August 1945 and the revolution had taken place. This time they met in the "North Vietnam Palace." Uncle inquired solicitously whether Hoang, who had just arrived in Hanoi, had everything he needed. "Where are you staying? Have you had a meal? Are you all right for clothes?" He was as simple and friendly as in the past, Hoang fondly recalls; not like the Head of State but the same old "Uncle." Though he lived in the splendid "North Vietnamese Palace" adorned with pictures, photos, standing mirrors and valuable old vases, he wore only a shirt, a pair of khaki trousers and white rubber sandals. Taking a packet of ready-made cigarettes from his pocket, he lit one for himself, put the rest in my breast pocket and buttoned it up. He still remembered that I was the hairdresser who now and then had bought some of these cigarettes for him.[110]

Early in 1941 Ho set up a base at Ching-hsi, a Chinese border town offering a convenient route into Vietnam. From Ching-hsi, Ho and his associates were able, without much difficulty, to slip across the border. Part of the journey was by sampan, which—as usual with any form of transportation in China—was so overcrowded that it offered cover to possible spies.[111] Ho, therefore, pretended to be a Chinese press correspondent speaking French:

Dong was his interpreter, and everybody took him for a journalist. The boat was going upstream and had to be pulled. Uncle took part in pulling the boat.[112] He only answered questions when translated to him. A certain Vietnamese woman, being thirsty, was about to drink river water. Ho told her in French, with Dong interpreting, "Don't drink that or you'll get stomach-ache, chew on sugar-cane instead." But when one of our comrades had his coat burnt by a cigarette, Uncle forgot his cover and called in Vietnamese, "Mind the fire!" Later, we used to have a good laugh over this story.[113]

Vo Nguyen Giap, later to become the top general of the Vietminh, also describes their life at this time:

From our cave we could see here and there sheets of limpid water, and a stream meandering round the mountain base. Uncle called it the Lenin stream. Every day he woke early and stirred up all of us. After physical exercise, he usually took a bath before starting work, despite the cold weather. He always kept himself busy—he either worked, held meetings, studied, gathered firewood or visited the nearby villages. Sometimes he organized a political training course for the old people or taught the children to read and write. If he did not go out he worked all day long at his "desk," a flat rock near the stream, and would stop only for meals. At night we slept on beds made of branches which of course were neither soft nor warm. It was very cold at night. Sometimes we had to make a fire and sit around it until daybreak. During these hours, Uncle would tell us the history of the world's people who had lived through many wars and revolutions. He foretold that within four or five years, the war in our country would enter its decisive phase and that would be a very favorable time for our revolution.[114]

Poems

Poetry is an integral element of the *chun tzu*. Ho did not write poetry for poetry's sake, he also employed messages in his poetry.

Old Sayings Explain Materialistic Concepts

On four important occasions Ho Chi Minh quoted a very old and widely known saying: *Co thuc moi duoc dao* (One must eat to be able to discharge one's duty). The word *dao* means the "way" or "religion." The word *vuc* means "uplift." The saying, in other words, supported the Marxist affirmation that "life is not determined by consciousness, but consciousness by life."[115]

To explain the determining material influences in molding people's consciousness, he used the proverb: *O bau thi tron, o ong thi dai* (Living in a gourd, one gets to be round; living in a tube, one gets to be long). To convey the importance of historical analysis, he relied on the saying: *Uong nuoc nho nguon* (Drink water, remember the source). To illustrate the relationship between action and reaction, he would say: *Vo quyt day mong tay nhon* (Thick-peeled mandarin, sharp nails).[116]

Popular Terms Clarify Basic Political Directives

In his "Letter to the People's Executive Committees," dated October 1945, and in characterizing one of the major mistakes committed by cadres—the breach of law—Ho Chi Minh used the terms: *Tu thu* and *tu oan* (Personal enmity and personal vengeance). The actual meaning can be approximated as: "Sometimes, because of personal enmity and rancor, you arrest honest people." Still, the translation misses the precision, the clarity and the strength of the original.

To condemn the refusal to admit mistakes, Ho resorted to the popular admonition: *Che thi chet, net khong chua* (Even dead, still keep the character). To describe exploitation, Ho characterized the imperialists: *Ngoi mat an bat vang* (Stay in a cool place, eat a bowl of gold). To expose the disparity between theory and practice, he would say: *Trong danh xuoi, ken thoi nguoc* (Drum beats one direction, clarinet blows the opposite).[117]

Ca Dao (Free Songs) Evoke the Popular Wisdom

Ho used an old, humorous, popular *Ca Dao* to demonstrate his conviction that the war of resistance against the French would be won, despite France's strength:

Nay Tuy Chau dau voi (Today the locust fights the elephant)
Nhung mai voi se bi loi rout ra (But tomorrow the elephant will be disemboweled)

The meaning is accurate but the martial music and the humor are lost. Ho Chi
Minh stressed the "mass line."

De muoi lan khong dan cung chiu (Ten times easy, without people, still impossible;)
Kho tram lan dan lieu cung xong (Hundred times difficult, people work at it,
   still accomplished)

The following *Ca Dao* originated from a song that propagated the Ten Point
Program of the Viet Minh Front formed in 1941:

Co muoi chinh sach bay ra (Ten policies are mapped out;)
Mot la ich quoc hai la loi dan (First useful to the country, second to the people)[118]

To hold the attention of Vietnamese audiences, it is essential to use the oral
forms of poetry with grace and ease. Ho Chi Minh was very successful in this
technique. His "Twelve Recommendations" list Six Forbiddances and Six Per-
missibles and end in a poem:

The above-mentioned twelve recommendations
are feasible to all.
He who loves his country
Will never forget them.
When the people have a habit
All are like one man.
With good armymen and good people,
Everything will be crowned with success.
Only when the root is firm, can the tree live long,
And victory is built with the people as foundation.

Poems from a Prison Diary

"Poems from a Prison Diary"[119] contains about one hundred short poems, all
very simple, charged with emotion, direct, and either anecdotal or moralistic.
Often, peasant humor will suddenly be replaced by the didacticism of the model
militant, adding that human warmth is combined with a stoicism that is typi-
cally Vietnamese.

From the very first words, we know what his moral standpoint was:

It is your body which is in prison,
not your mind ...

And we know that the importance he attaches to his poems is relative:

I versify until such time as I shall see freedom.

But the tone becomes more elevated, shifting from anecdote to points of morality:

> The rice-grain suffers under the pestle;
> yet admire its whiteness when the ordeal is over.
> It is the same with human beings in our time—
> to be a man, you must endure the pestle of misfortune.

Or again, as he watches his fellow prisoners sleeping, covered with lice:

> Eyes closed, they all look honest and pure.
> Waking divides them into evil and good.
> Good, evil—no one is either by nature.
> It is what you become, mainly through upbringing.

Sometimes a cry of pain escapes him:

> Four inhuman months
> in the depths of this jail.
> More than ten years' aging
> has ravaged my body!

Or else he dreams, tenderly at first:

> The rose blossoms and the rose
> withers without awareness of what
> it does. The scent of a rose has only
> to stray into a prison
> for all the world's injustices
> to shriek within the prisoner's heart.

The dream has turned into an indictment:

> The poems of our day must be clad in steel.
> Poets too must know how to fight!

At one moment he is full of longing, at another full of barbs:

> In the morning the sun climbs the wall
> and comes knocking on the door; the door stays shut;
> night still tarries in the depths of the prison....
> Being chained is a luxury to compete for.
> The chained have somewhere to sleep,
> the unchained haven't ...
> The State treats me to its rice, I lodge in its palaces,
> its guards take turns escorting me.
> Really, the honor is too great.

Reinhold Neumann-Hoditz writes that for Ho prison was certainly the most difficult of his whole life. With his hands and feet shackled, chained together with bandits, he was dragged from prison to prison for fourteen months. Neumann-Hoditz continues by saying that Ho wrote his four-line verses and poems in Mandarin Chinese and the Vietnamese style *Tuc Tuyet*. (He wrote them in Mandarin Chinese so as not to arouse the distrust of his guards, working during the endless nights when he could not sleep.)[120]

Often the prisoners covered more than thirty miles on foot in a single day before they reached a new prison. Sometimes they were loaded onto junks.

> Carried along by the current, the boat glides towards Nanning.
> Our legs are tied to the roof, as though we were on gallows.
> Along both banks of the river are lively prosperous villages.
> The boats of the fishermen glide swiftly in mid-stream.[121]

Despite his harsh treatment, Ho attempted to bear his fate with dignity.

> The supple rope has now been replaced with iron fetters.
> At every step they jingle as though I wore jade rings.
> In spite of being a prisoner, accused of being a spy,
> I move with all the dignity of an ancient government official.[122]

But he was depressed and cursed the fate that condemned him to inaction.

> The whole world is ablaze with flames of war,
> And men compete as to who will be the first at the front.
> In jail inaction weighs heavily on the prisoner.
> My noble ambitions are valued at less than a cent.[123]

Ho commented sarcastically in verse on the fate of some of his fellow prisoners and conditions in general in China.

"The Wife of the Deserter"

> One day you went away, not to come back again,
> Leaving me alone in our room, with sadness for companion.
> The authorities having pity on my loneliness,
> Invited me to live temporarily in the prison.[124]

"The Child in Pin Yang Prison"

> Oh, oh! oh! My father's run away,
> My father is afraid to be a soldier.
> So I'm in Prison, though I'm only six months old.
> I had to come with my mother.[125]

After a year's detention, Ho Chi Minh penned the following poem:

"Autumn Night"

My heart travels a thousand li towards my native land.
My dream intertwines with sadness like a skein of a
thousand threads.
Innocent, I have now endured a whole year in prison.
Using my tears for ink, I turn my thoughts into verses.[126]

"Hard Is the Road to Life"

Having climbed over steep mountains and high peaks,
How should I expect on the plains to meet greater danger?
In the mountains, I met a tiger and came out unscathed,
On the plains, I encountered men, and was thrown into prison.
I was a representative of Viet-Nam
On my way to China to meet an important personage.
On the quiet road a sudden storm broke loose,
And I was thrust into jail as an honored guest.
I am a straightforward man, with no crime on my conscience,
But I was accused of being a spy for China.
So life, you see, is never a very smooth business,
And now the present bristles with difficulties.[127]

It was soon after this imprisonment that Ho's comrades learned of his arrest. Indeed, the day came when they were informed of his death, which—like his earlier "death" in Hong Kong eleven years before—was accepted without challenge for months afterward.[128]

Vo Nguyen Giap relates this episode with wit and feeling:

One day I received a letter from Pham Van Dong ... informing me that Uncle Ho had just died in the jails of the Kuomintang. We were almost paralyzed with grief. We organized a ceremony of commemoration for our revered leader, and Comrade Dong was given the task of writing his funeral oration. We opened Uncle's rattan case in search of mementos. One of our comrades was dispatched to China, with orders to locate his grave.... A few months later we received a newspaper mailed from China. On the wrapper were a few lines in verse in a hand which was well known to us:

The clouds are setting the peaks aglow,
The peaks are hugging the clouds—
I wander alone, roused to feeling,
Scanning the distant southern sky:
I am thinking of my friends.

We were wild with joy, and no less astonished. We fired question after question to Comrade Dong, who had brought the sad news to us. "But," he insisted, "the Chinese governor told me: '*Su Liu!* (Already dead!)'" "No, no, your ear confused the tonic accents; what he must have said was '*Chu Liu! Chu Liu!* (Very fit!).'"[129]

In summary, Ho was looked upon by the peasantry in Vietnam as a *chun tzu*, or a sage leader as defined by their culture. He gained the respect of the Vietnamese people because of his substantive themes and arguments for equality and freedom on their behalf and because of the development of his character and his lifelong behavior.

NOTES

1. Ho Chi Minh, *Poems from a Prison Diary* (Hanoi: Foreign Languages Publishing House, 1959).

2. John C. Hammerback, "Jose Antonio's Rhetoric of Fascism," *Southern Journal of Communication* 3 (1994), 183.

3. Ho Chi Minh, *The Selected Works of Ho Chi Minh* (Hanoi: Foreign Languages Publishing House), 53.

4. Jean Lacouture states that when the Versailles Peace Conference started work, Ho and his friend Phan Van Troung—aided by the Phan Chu Trinh—drew up an eight-point program for their country's emancipation and forwarded it to the conference secretariat in January 1919. This plan had been inspired by President Wilson's Fourteen Points. See Jean Lacouture, *Ho Chi Minh: A Political Biography* (New York: Random House, 1968), 24.

5. Ibid., 25.

6. For the complete text, see Appendix A.

7. See Ho Chi Minh, "Report on the National and Colonial Questions at the Fifth Congress of the Communist International," in Bernard Fall, *Ho Chi Minh on Revolution: Selected Writings, 1920–66* (New York: Frederick A. Praeger, 1967), 57–67.

8. *Thanh Nien* (Youth) is the current abbreviation of the term *Viet-Nam Thanh-Nien Cach-Menh Dong-Chi Hoi* (the Association of Vietnamese Revolutionary Young Comrades). The word *Dong Chi* (in Chinese *T'ung Chi*), meaning "comrade," reflects the Communist tendency of the movement. This is the first occasion of its use in the Vietnamese language. This was the name that Ho Chi Minh gave to a crypto-Communist organization that he founded in Canton in 1925, a few months after he had been sent there by the Comintern. See Hoang Van Chi, *From Colonialism to Communism: A Case History of North Vietnam* (New York: Frederick A. Praeger, 1964), 42.

9. Ho taught in Thanh Nien and wrote *Duong Cach Menh*. For the complete text, see Appendix A.

10. Thomas Hodgkin, *Vietnam: The Revolutionary Path* (London: Macmillan, 1981), 225–226.

11. Ibid.

12. The original appeal was drafted in English and later translated into Vietnamese. There is some dispute as to whether the Party's original name was the Vietnamese Communist Party or the Communist Party of Indochina, the title the Internationale had proscribed. That name was, in fact, adopted at a second meeting held in October 1930.

13. See Ho Chi Minh, "The Party's Line in the Period of the Democratic Front (1936–39)," in Fall, *Ho Chi Minh on Revolution*, 130.

14. The Eighth Plenum of the Central Committee of the Communist Party of Indochina, held at Pac Bo (Coo Bang province) 10–19 May 1941, decided on a new line highlighting the slogan "national liberation," establishing the Viet Minh Front, changing the names of various mass organizations into Associations for National Salvation, and speed-

ing up the preparations for an abortive armed uprising against the French on 6 June 1941. This letter calls on revolutionary fighters at home, together with all other Vietnamese, to rise up and overthrow the Japanese and the French. See Fall, *Ho Chi Minh on Revolution*, 132.

15. The National Congress held on 16 August 1945, at Tan Trao (Tuyen Quang province), was called by the Viet Minh Central Committee. The conference was convened so hastily that few non-Vietminh organizations had an opportunity to express their views. The Congress approved the ten policies and the order of general insurrection issued by the Viet Minh Front and appointed the Viet-Nam National Liberation Committee, which was in fact the Provisional Government of the Democratic Republic of Viet-Nam, presided over by Ho Chi Minh. After the closing of the Congress, Ho wrote "An Appeal for General Insurrection" calling on the Vietnamese people to rise up and regain their independence. See Fall, *Ho Chi Minh on Revolution*, 41.

16. Ibid., 141–142.

17. Lacouture, *Ho Chi Minh*, 102.

18. Ellen Hammer, *Vietnam: Yesterday and Today* (New York: Holt, Rinehart and Winston, 1966), 134.

19. "Equality" became a word with multiple definitions. To the Confucians, it meant people equal to one another according to class rank, family, et cetera (although true equality never existed in the Confucian system); to the French, it meant the difference between French and Vietnamese, peasantry, land ownership, et cetera. Ho chose to avoid the ambiguity of the word.

20. The rhetoric of the early 1920s regarding equality appears to have been abandoned, although Ho's use of equality referred mainly to equality between nationalities more than individuals.

21. Hue-Tam Ho Tai, *Radicalism and the Origins of the Vietnamese Revolution* (Cambridge: Harvard University Press, 1992), 256.

22. Bernard Fall, *Last Reflections of a War* (Garden City, N.Y.: Doubleday, 1967), 72.

23. The production of rice-alcohol was the monopoly of a French firm, the *Societe des Distilleries de l'Indochine*, whose products were so bad that the Vietnamese preferred to drink their own distilled alcoholic concoctions. To safeguard the French firm's interests, the government made frequent raids on Vietnamese property, imposing heavy fines and imprisonment. Despite these stringent measures, the private production of alcohol persisted. In the end, the government adopted the policy of distributing a fixed quantity of "official" alcohol to every village, obliging the inhabitants to pay for it. See Hoang, *From Colonialism to Communism*, n.7, 39.

24. Nguyen Ai Quoc, "Speech At The Tours Congress," *Writings of Ho Chi Minh*. Also see Lacouture, *Ho Chi Minh*, 27–28. For the complete speech, see Appendix A.

25. Fall, *Last Reflections of a War*, 72.

26. The quotations from *Le Proces de la Colonisation Francaise* are from Charles Fenn's translations in his *Oeuvres Choisies* (Hanoi: Foreign Languages Publishing House, 1960), 1:195f. For Ho's quote, see Charles Fenn, *Ho Chi Minh: A Biographical Introduction* (New York: Charles Scribner's Sons, 1973), 29.

27. Fenn, *Ho Chi Minh*, 29.

28. Fall, *Ho Chi Minh on Revolution*, vi–xi.

29. Also translated as "Reflections on the Colonial Question."

30. Fenn, *Ho Chi Minh*, 36.

31. For the complete text, see Appendix A.

32. Fenn, *Ho Chi Minh*, 37.

33. A native of a French colony; a French Communist persecuted by the colonists.

34. For the complete text, see Appendix A.

35. For the complete text, see Appendix A.

36. For the complete text, see Appendix A.

37. See Ho Chi Minh, "An Appeal from the Peasant International to the Working Peasants in the Colonies," in Fall, *Ho Chi Minh on Revolution*, 118.

38. Osip Mandel'stam, "Nguyen Ai Quoc—A Meeting with an International Communist," *Plamya* 36 (23 December 1923); reprinted in *Hoc Tap* 6 (June 1970), 37–42. Article located at the Indochina Archives, University of California, Berkeley, California, File DRV, Subj BIOG, Date June 1970, Sub-cat. Ho Chi Minh.

39. For the complete text, see Appendix A.

40. Located at the Indochina Archives, University of California, Berkeley, California, File DRV, Subj BIOG, Date March 1924, Sub-cat. Ho Chi Minh.

41. The conference was held from 12 November 1921 to 6 February 1922. Attendees were from the United States, the United Kingdom, Japan, France, Italy, China, Belgium, Portugal, and the Netherlands.

42. Hodgkin, *Vietnam*, 225.

43. Ibid., 225.

44. Hammer, *Vietnam*, 134.

45. Ho Chi Minh, Located in the Indochina Archives, University of California, Berkeley, California, File DRV, Subj BIOG, Date July 1939, Sub-cat. Ho Chi Minh. "Appeal Made by Comrade Nguyen Ai Quoc on the Occasion of the Founding of the Party," 3 February 1930.

46. Hammerback, "Jose Antonio's Rhetoric of Fascism," 183.

47. Frederick J. Antczak, *Thought and Character: The Rhetoric of Democratic Education* (Ames: Iowa State University Press, 1985), 11.

48. Ibid.

49. Maurice Charland thoroughly explains how through rhetorical identification, discourse can constitute an audience and motivate it to enact an ideological agenda. See Maurice Charland, "Constitutive Rhetoric: *The Case of the Peuple* Quebecois," *Quarterly Journal of Speech* 2 (1987), 133–150. For further explanation of the view that rhetorical discourse can stimulate an audience to behave in ways not characteristic of its individual members, see Michael McGee ("In Search of 'The People,' *Quarterly Journal of Speech* 3 [1975], 235–249), who in the course of his essay notes that Hitler asserted that each of history's powerful "reform" movements required a great leader to translate the longings of individuals into a collective group and who would in turn mirror that group.

50. Edwin Black, "The Second Persona," *Quarterly Journal of* Speech 2 (1970), 113.

51. Hammerback, "Jose Antonio's Rhetoric of Fascism," 186.

52. Ibid.

53. Ibid.

54. Charland, "Constitutive Rhetoric," 133.

55. Ho Chi Minh, "Lenin and the Peoples of the East," Le Paria, July 27, 1924, located at the Indochina Archives, file DRV, BIOG, subj., date 7/24/ , sub-cat HO, University of California, Berkeley.

56. Appeal Made BY Comrade Nguyen Ai Quoc On The Occasion Of The Founding Of The Party, 3 February, 1930, [Hanoi Domestic Service in Vietnamese, 0430 GMT, 28 May 1971], located at the Indochina Archives, file DRV, BIOG, subj., date 2/30/ , sub-cat Ho Chi Minh, University of California, Berkeley.

57. Ho Chi Minh, "The Line of the Party during the Period of the Democratic Front (1936–1939)," *Tuyen Tap*, July 1939. Reprinted by Su That Publishing House, Hanoi, 1960, pp. 196. Located in the Indochina Archives, University of California, Berkeley, California, File DRV, Subj BIOG, Date July 1939, Sub-cat. Ho Chi Minh.

58. Hoang, *From Colonialism to Communism*, 43–44.

59. In 1284, Kubilai Khan, the Mongol emperor, tried to force Vietnam into submission. He sent an army of five hundred thousand men to conquer Vietnam. The Vietnamese emperor sent his best general, Tran Hung Dao, to drive out the invaders. A master in guerrilla warfare, General Tran Hung Dao opted for a superb defense strategy and effective tactics to overcome his inferiority in number of troops and weapons. Three hundred and fifty years earlier, General Ngo Quyen used the underwater spikes to defeat the Chinese. Now, General Tran Hung Dao employed a similar strategy; and history repeated itself. With this victory, Tran established his dynasty after the death of the ruling emperor. See Pham Kim Vinh, *The Vietnamese Culture: An Introduction* (San Diego, Calif.: Pham Kim Vinh Research Institute, 1990), 22–23.

60. Charland, "Constitutive Rhetoric," 143.

61. Ibid.

62. Hammerback, "Jose Antonio's Rhetoric of Fascism," 186.

63. In 1898 the French passed a law suppressing freedom of press in Vietnam. Patriotic literature—poems, anecdotes, and narratives—were circulated clandestinely by word of mouth or written in characters and then communicated orally to the masses. Chinese and Chu Nom remained the exclusive writing system of the resistance. For further detail, see John DeFrancis, *Colonialism and Language Policy in Vietnam* (The Hague: Mouton Publishers, 1977), 154–155.

64. Osip Mandel'stam, *Plamya* 36 (23 December 1923), translator: Documentation Office, *Hoc Tap*, Article: Hanoi, *Hoc Tap*, Vietnamese, No. 6, June 70, pp. 37–42. This document is located at the Indochina Archives, File DRV, Subj BIOG, Sub-cat Ho Chi Minh, University of California, Berkeley, California.

65. Ho Chi Minh, *Poems from a Prison Diary* (Hanoi: Foreign Languages Publishing House, 1959).

66. Robert Shaplen, *The Lost Revolution* (New York: Harper and Row, 1965), 62.

67. Hoang, *From Colonialism to Communism*, ix.

68. William Warby, *Ho Chi Minh and the Struggle for an Independent Vietnam* (London: Merlin, 1972), 111.

69. Bui Lam, *Days with Ho Chi Minh* (Hanoi: Foreign Languages Publishing House, 1965), 48.

70. Warby, *Ho Chi Minh*, 8.

71. Hodgkin, *Vietnam*, 224.

72. Ibid.

73. Reinhold Neumann-Hoditz, *Portrait of Ho Chi Minh: An Illustrated Biography*, trans. John Hargreaves (Hamburg: Herder and Herder, 1972), 129.

74. Sun Tzu was a famous strategist of the third century B.C. whose military precepts are still respected. In an offensive action, Sun Tzu recommended three operations: "First conquer the heart (of the people), second conquer (the source of) supplies, and thirdly conquer the fortresses." Looking back on the War of Resistance, it is apparent that the Vietminh observed the first principle. See Hoang, *From Colonialism to Communism*, 66.

75. See also Lacouture, *Ho Chi Minh*, 78.

76. Lacouture

77. Ho Chi Minh, "Letter to Graduating Students," located in the Indochina Archives, University of California, Berkeley, California, File DRV, Subj BIOG, Date September 1945, Sub-cat Ho Chi Minh.

78. Hoang Van Chi joined the Vietnamese resistance movement at the outset. During his years with the movement, he had observed firsthand much of what he wrote about. He later sympathized with South Vietnam in the 1960s. See Hoang, *From Colonialism to Communism*, x.

79. According to Hoang, Ho took a Chinese wife while in Hong Kong and had a daughter by her, but that in 1949, he asked the Chinese Communist Party to make inquiries as to her whereabouts, but no trace of this woman could be found.

80. Cited in Hoang, *From Colonialism to Communism*, 33–35.

81. Warby, *Ho Chi Minh*, 8.

82. Warby, *Ho Chi Minh*, 8.

83. Ibid.

84. Ibid., 110.

85. Ibid., 110–113.

86. David Halberstam, *Ho* (New York: Random House, 1971), 12–13.

87. Ibid., 13.

88. The simplest American view of Asians that *Time* magazine exemplified was applied to its Asian heroes such as Boa Dai as well. Thus, in October 1946: "'You ask him kill bird,' said foxy little Annamite Louis Ko. 'He no like. He like kill big.' Press agent Louis was speaking of his master, tall, strapping, Paris-educated Boa Dai who once killed 10 elephants in three days and captured one single handed.'" Cited in Halberstam, *Ho*, 13.

89. Ibid., 14–15.

90. Ibid., 14.

91. Ibid., 18.

92. Ibid., 17.

93. Fenn, *Ho Chi Minh*, 46.

94. Ibid.

95. Tran Ngoc Danh, quoting Ho in *Histoire du President Ho* (Hanoi: Foreign Languages Publishing House, 1949), 33. Cited in Fenn, *Ho Chi Minh*, 46.

96. Fenn, *Ho Chi Minh*, 46.

97. Ibid., 46.

98. Jean Sainteny, *Ho Chi Minh and His Vietnam: A Personal Memoir* (Chicago: Cowles Book Company, 1972), 130.

99. Neumann-Hoditz, *Portrait of Ho Chi Minh: An Illustrated Biography*, 169.

100. Ibid.

101. Ibid., 9.

102. Ibid., 170.

103. Shaplen, *The Lost Revolution*, 70.

104. Ibid., 47–48.

105. Cited in Fenn, *Ho Chi Minh*, 40.

106. "Ho" is a fairly common Chinese name that the Vietnamese leader had already used when going to Yenan. See Fenn, *Ho Chi Minh*, 70.

107. See Bui, *Days with Ho Chi Minh*, 138–139.

108. See ibid., 140.

109. See ibid., 147–148.

110. See ibid., 148.

111. Fenn, *Ho Chi Minh*, 66–67.

112. According to Fenn, Ho seems to have made a point of taking, whenever possible, a physical role: he pulls sampans, pushes carts, chops wood, fetches food, washes children, cleans rooms, performs exercises, cooks meals, and cultivates gardens. By challenging his physique in this fashion, he no doubt accumulated a "sack full of diamonds" against the severe hardship of his later life. See Fenn, *Ho Chi Minh*, 67.

113. Ibid., 67.

114. Cited in *Days with Ho Chi Minh*, 186–187.

115. Tran Van Dinh, "The Rhetoric of Revolt: Ho Chi Minh as Communicator," *Journal of Communication* 26, no. 4 (1976), 142.

116. Ibid., 143.

117. Ibid., 143–144.

118. Ibid., 144.

119. Ho Chi Minh, "Poems from a Prison Diary," cited in Fall, *Ho Chi Minh on Revolution*, 135.

120. Neumann-Hoditz, *Portrait of Ho Chi Minh*, 137.

121. Ibid., 137–138.

122. Ibid., 138.

123. Ibid.

124. Ibid., 139.

125. Ibid., 139.

126. Ibid., 139.

127. Ibid. 139

128. Lacouture, *Ho Chi Minh*, 79.

129. See Appendix A for the original version of the poem included in this extract. Lacouture, *Ho Chi Minh*, 79–80.

6

Conclusions

INDEPENDENCE

Neither high, nor very far,
Neither emperor, nor king,
You are only a little milestone,
Which stands at the edge of the highway.
To people passing by
You point the right direction,
And stop them from getting lost.
You tell them of the distance
For which they still must journey
Your service is not a small one.
And people will always remember you.[1]

By August of 1945, the Vietnamese had been looking for a sign of a new order, when Ho Chi Minh emerged to proclaim the independence of Vietnam.[2] Since 1943, he had calmed the impatience of supporters of premature insurrection by telling them "we must wait for the propitious moment"[3]—this moment had now arrived.[4] On 19 August, the Vietminh forces entered Hanoi and took control, firing only a few symbolic revolver shots in the process.[5] The "August Revolution" crowned with success the democratic and national aspirations voiced by the Vietminh since 1941.[6]

The news of the successful Hanoi insurrection quickly spread throughout the country.[7] On 25 August, Bao Dai publicly announced his abdication to the throne, which not only saved his life but also induced Ho Chi Minh to grant him an honorific position as supreme adviser to the first republican government.[8] On 29 August, exactly two weeks after the Japanese surrender and five days after the abdication of Emperor Bao Dai, Ho announced the formation of a Provisional Government[9] and proclaimed himself president.[10] On 30 August, Emperor Bao Dai thus became citizen Vinh Thuy, thereby, not only Bao Dai, but the whole Nguyen dynasty, lost its throne.[11]

From the point of view of the common man in the rice field the abdication of Emperor Bao Dai was an important event.[12] This was especially true because he declared that he wanted to enter the ranks of this newly constituted people as a "plain" individual. How easy of them to imagine that in these events was an expression of the power of the new system, a revolutionary "virtue" supported by a new world in conflict with the old order.[13] In deferring to the revolutionaries, the monarchy publicly claimed that its alliance with France had been the cause of its downfall, but this abdication was thought by the people to be a sign of heavenly decision, which would result in France being driven from Vietnam.[14]

The seizure of power was astonishingly nonviolent, an almost bloodless insurrection. The Vietminh were brought to power, but without having defeated any enemies.[15]

Consequently, from the very moment in 1945 that the supporters of the revolutionary party changed over from the position of dissenters to a mastery of the situation, they were expected to eliminate all the elements of the former system; compromises were not anticipated.[16] Eliminated by the new government were the councils of notables. This measure was *the* major act in the domestic history of the Democratic Republic of Vietnam.[17] This decision had been provoked by two considerations. First, a broad and systematic national policy found expression in the immediate replacement of the customary councils by a new type of village committee. Second, in support of these new committees there was a regrouping of Vietnamese village society in a pattern that was radically different from its traditional structure.[18] By providing peasant villagers with new forms of political participation, political status, and equality, the Vietminh bridged the gaps between the relatively nonmodernized areas of Vietnamese society, creating a new sense of community. Although the doctrine of the Vietminh was not known in detail, it hardly mattered, since the doctrine had only to make a general impression on the minds of the people, who could then take a position for or against it. At the end of August, the Vietminh flag was flying on the Chinese border and the Camau peninsula.[19]

On 2 September, at the very moment the Japanese were officially signing the capitulation on the aircraft carrier *Missouri*, the independent republic of Vietnam was declared. The "Mandate from Heaven" had been given to the Vietminh. The relinquishing of the great state seal to Provisional Government representatives by Bao Dai confirmed the legitimacy of the new power. The previously accepted imperial order had collapsed within the space of a few hours and became a thing of the past.[20] The transfer of the "Mandate from Heaven" from one authority to the other in the best Confucian tradition and the August revolution initially seemed to confirm the national de facto situation.[21] For the first time in eighty-three years, a Vietnamese government was in a position to direct the affairs of the whole country in complete independence.[22]

INDEPENDENCE DAY

Archimedes Patti recalls that the first Sunday in September was the Feast of Vietnamese Martyrs; it was also the day selected by Ho Chi Minh as Independence Day. All the people of Hanoi and the surrounding districts were summoned to attend a mass assembly in Ba Dinh Square that afternoon.[23] Before a cheering audience of more than five hundred thousand people, Ho, appearing before his compatriots for the first time under that name, proclaimed the end of French colonial rule in Vietnam. He announced the creation of the sovereign, independent Democratic Republic of Vietnam with himself as President-Designate, and declared that the authority of the Provisional Government of the Democratic Republic of Vietnam, of which he was the acting head, must be obeyed throughout the entire territory of Vietnam.[24]

Hoang Van Chi recalls that the assembly did not know this person who called himself Ho Chi Minh, nor did they know where he came from or by what authority he claimed the presidency. As Ho began his speech, word spread throughout the audience that Ho Chi Minh was none other than Nguyen Ai Quoc—(Nguyen the Patriot), a name that was already a legend to the Vietnamese. Thus, by his moral standing alone, Ho acquired the respect and confidence of the entire Vietnamese nation. His reputation for honesty and sincerity contributed greatly to his success. He was the beaming father figure of his people, the man of constant simplicity. This was the great nationalist who reflected the traditions and aspirations of his people.[25]

Ho Chi Minh stood smiling, diminutive in size but gigantic in the adulation of his people. Raising his hands in a paternal gesture, he called for silence and began his now-famous proclamation with the words: "All men are created equal. The Creator has given us certain inviolable Rights; the right to Life, the right to be Free, and the right to achieve Happiness."[26] As skillfully as Ho began his speech, he concluded with the words: "Vietnam has the right to enjoy freedom and independence, and in fact, has become a free and independent nation. The whole Vietnamese people is resolved to bring all its spirit and its power, its life, and its possessions to preserve this right to freedom and independence."[27] Ho also emphasized how the French had lost their mandate as "protector" through their subservience to Japan.[28]

When Ho entered Hanoi in 1945 and, upon his declaration of independence, addressed his own people for the first time, he said, "I can't tell you what you have to do [to achieve nationhood] but I can show it to you." He put his thumb on the table. "If everywhere you put your thumb on the sacred earth of Vietnam, and a plant will grow, then we will succeed. If not, we will fail."[29] Paul Mus, the French expert on Vietnam, who witnessed the scene, was struck by the fact that this man who had been absent so long had lost no feel or touch for the life of a peasant:

He was on the one hand a Marxist economist who knows the importance of the basic production and on the other hand a Confucian scholar, because what you must keep in mind is the idea that the thumb on the earth is a simple Chinese proverb—a thumb-square of planting rice is more precious than a thumb-square of gold. So you can see how Ho Chi Minh in that situation was directly in contact with the millions of peasants in the rice fields, who at the sight of him were ready to give all their strength, all their devotion to the nation, and if needed, their blood."[30]

Ellen Hammer supports this: "Since the beginning of their recorded history the Vietnamese have built their lives around their rice fields. Rice was not only their daily food but was one of the ritual offerings which the Vietnamese made to their gods and ancestors."[31]

McAlister and Mus aptly describe the relationship between the rice field and the peasant: "At the very foundation of Vietnamese society the rice fields have throughout history supplied this society with a reason for being. The fields have provided the basis for a stable structure, a discipline for work, and a rhythm of communal celebrations—in short, a contract between the society itself, the soil, and the sky."[32]

CONCLUSION

The old proverb *Phep vua thua le lang* (the laws of the emperor yield to the customs of the village) is known by all Vietnamese. In many respects it characterizes the village in Vietnam as a self-contained homogeneous community, jealously guarding its way of life—a little world that is autonomous and disregards (if not disdains) the outside world.[33]

The Vietnamese share a cosmological view deeply rooted in the Buddhist–Taoist–Confucianist ideology of the Chinese Great Tradition, with Vietnamese alterations and additions, which underlies the amalgam of beliefs and practices that make up village religion, and it influences all other aspects of village society as well.[34] Adherence to it is manifest in behavior almost daily. Belief in universal order, and the related concepts of harmony with this order and human destiny within it, are reflected in the way all villagers conform to guidance by the lunar calendar and reliance on individual horoscopy, and in the respect most villagers have for the principles of geomancy.[35] The notion of harmony is involved in many practices and rituals: observance of taboos, use of amulets or talismans, preparation of medicines, consultation with healers, propitiation or expulsion of spirits, invocations to deities, and veneration of ancestors. The aim is to preserve or restore harmony and, with it, well-being.[36]

There also is homogeneity in the social expectation. The drive to provide well for one's family combined with some of the basic beliefs associated with the Cult of the Ancestors contributes to the strong motivation for economic gain that characterizes the Vietnamese peasant (which in turn has contributed to the expansionism that marks Vietnamese history).[37]

Most villagers want to improve their lot, which means having land, a fine house, material comforts, and education for one's children. A concern that the Vietnamese have for poverty is that the family may disintegrate as members quit the village to seek a livelihood elsewhere. For the villager it is extremely important that the family remain together: in addition to the comfort of having kinfolk about, immortality lies in an undying lineage.[38]

The experience of conquest for Vietnam was by no means novel. Vietnam as a people, a nation, and a culture had been forged over two millennia of resistance against Chinese domination. To survive, the Vietnamese had borrowed freely from Chinese social, political, and cultural institutions and values. But the new enemy from the West (France) posed a different challenge.[39]

In equating independence with survival, patriotic literati believed that they were engaged in a desperate race against annihilation as a people and a culture. Their country appeared to them to be a *nhuoc tieu* (weak and small) nation in the process of being swallowed up by a stronger and fitter France.[40] Language reinforced this cannibalistic vision of colonialism as a *che do thuc dan* (people-eating system), an even more evocative description than the usual "dog-eat-dog" metaphors of Social Darwinism.[41] Accustomed as they were to employing cultural yardsticks to measure national health, these literati opted to follow the path already taken by their Chinese counterparts in attempting to strengthen their country by reforming its culture. But the zeal of the Vietnamese literati in embracing what they called "new learning" from the West compounded the profound changes that colonialism had brought to the political, economic, and social landscape of Vietnam.[42] It also undermined the power of Confucian orthodoxy and the moral authority of tradition. The very language used by these literati was not uniform. In the south, French was used even by those who sought to overthrow French rule. In other regions, older anticolonial activists stuck to Chinese. Increasingly, however, the Vietnamese vernacular, in its Romanized writing system—once despised as a tool of the invaders—was employed by enemies and upholders of the colonial order alike. But whether written in Vietnamese, Chinese, or French, many of the words were unfamiliar; others were old terms that had been given new meanings and a different resonance. They became weapons in a struggle for control over ruling metaphors and symbols. Both friends and foes of change used the rhetoric of the family, the metaphor of adolescence and immaturity, and, above all, the emblematic figure of Vietnamese womanhood to illustrate their particular vision of both present and future.[43]

For Ho Chi Minh, revolution came to seem the only possible solution to an existential predicament that bound his personal concerns to those of the nation in a tight and seemingly natural unity. He saw a symmetry between the national struggle for independence from colonial rule and his efforts to emancipate his people from the oppressiveness of French social institutions. He knew well enough that the audience he must reach consisted, in the main, of tradition-bound peasants.[44] Ho's revolutionary discourse of the 1920s fundamentally changed the literati's revolutionary discourse of radicalism and anarchism; this was done by the introduction of Marxism–Leninism.[45] Charles Fenn asserts that Ho perceived that his fellow countrymen suffered economically—they were the "have-nots" against the French "haves"—and Confucianism, Buddhism, and Christianity offered them small comfort and no relief.[46] Furthermore, the Vietnamese, like most Asians, were firm believers in Fate. The Marxist concept included the *inevitability* of proletarian victory. It is not without significance that the Vietnamese expression for revolution—*cach mang*—literally means "change fate." Whereas radicals conceived of independence as arising organically from their struggle toward self-emancipation, Ho's discourse established a new symmetry between national liberation and the pursuit of social justice along class lines.

To some, security was more important than freedom, predictability more desirable than perfection. This meant accepting inherited institutions, no matter how oppressive, and the colonial system, no matter how unjust. Others, however, were drawn to freedom because of its multiple meanings: liberation of the nation from colonial rule and emancipation of the individual from the patriarchal family system, outdated moral values, and authoritarian social institutions.[47] But the corollary of freedom was uncertainty, and even those committed to the revolutionary enterprise needed reassurance. Ready as they were to sacrifice the present to the future, they, too, sought certainty, albeit of another kind: not the belief that tomorrow would be like today, and therefore endurable, but the sure knowledge that it would be utterly different, and therefore better. Only then would their sacrifices and their transgressions against conventional morality not be in vain. Amid the vagaries of revolutionary life, Ho's promise of certain victory must have seemed irresistible. In the meantime, he balanced iron discipline with comradely warmth and acted as the substitute for the despised patriarchal family.[48]

Ho's literary romanticization of revolution, however devoid of real substance, helped restore sympathy for the revolutionary enterprise among the peasant class. This renewed sympathy made it possible for the rhetoric of kinship to recover its former resonance and to be put, finally, in the service of revolution. The power of this rhetoric was strikingly demonstrated soon after Ho declared Vietnam independent on 2 September 1945. Throughout his address, he chose to stress the theme of freedom rather than equality, which had come to symbolize class conflict and national disunity. But it was collective, not individual, freedom he was talking about, as his closing words made clear: "Vietnam has the right to enjoy freedom and independence, and in fact, has become a free and independent nation. The whole Vietnamese people is resolved to bring all its spirit and its power, its life, and its possessions to preserve this right to freedom and independence."[49]

In invoking Vietnam's ancestral legacy, Ho Chi Minh demonstrated that control of national symbols and metaphors had returned to the Vietnamese. Ho referred to himself by an appellation that became familiar worldwide: Uncle Ho. In thus implying kinship and solidarity with his audience, Ho showed that it was possible once again to extol intergenerational harmony and to put the evocative language of the family at the service of the nation. With this joining of piety and patriotism, the early phase of the Vietnamese Revolution was over.

Ho and the Vietminh were always sensitive to local nuance, always sensitive to Vietnamese tradition. A captured soldier was asked by interrogators: "When you joined the Front did you tell your family?" This, after all, was the critical question; the greatest loyalty is to the family. "No, I did not," he replied, "I felt it was my filial duty, but I talked to the Front and they said to me, 'Comrade, your words show that you are a fine son filled with filial piety and we admire that very much, but in the face of the loss and destruction of your country you have to choose between filial duty and duty toward your country. In this war the people are your family too, and you have to suffer. If you do your duty toward your parents—tell them of your decision—then you fail your country, then by the same act you will have completed your duty toward your family, because they will be free and no longer exploited.'"[50]

To the peasant, consigned by birth to a life of misery, poverty, and ignorance, Ho showed a way out. A man could be as good as his innate talent permitted; lack of privilege was for the first time in centuries not a handicap—if anything, it was an asset. One could fight and die serving the nation, liberating both the nation and oneself. Nepotism and privilege, which had dominated the feudal society of the past, were wiped away. One rose only on ability. And in putting all this extraordinary human machinery together, Ho gave a sense of nation to this formerly suspicious and fragmented society, until at last that which united the Vietnamese was more powerful than that which divided them—until they were in fact a nation, just as he had claimed.[51]

Hoang Van Chi notes that an important factor usually unnoticed by outside observers was the moral indignation generated in ordinary decent Vietnamese people by the corrupt practices sanctioned by the colonial regime.[52] This of itself was sufficient to stimulate very large numbers of them to support the revolution. Any rebels, no matter what ideology they supported, would have been regarded by these people as the courageous protagonists of right and justice. The mandarins serving the colonial administration, whose comfortable lives were made more conspicuous by the general poverty surrounding them, personified for the people not only treachery to the national cause but corruption and depravity as well. Revolutions may spring from many causes, but the Vietnamese revolution was motivated first by the people's eagerness to get rid of mandarinic despotism and insolence. For the Vietnamese people, the revolution was a conflict between virtue and vice. The ideological dispute that later developed was regarded as a complicating, but subsidiary, factor.

The conflict was between "virtue and vice."[53] Since the population of the countryside, where over 80 percent of the Vietnamese lived in 1945, was not united in any political community beyond the village, the prospects for either rallying the peasants against colonial rule or creating a new system of politics was limited. Moreover, the peasants, to the extent that they were anticipating some new indigenous political superstructure in Vietnam, were expecting a revival of traditional forms of politics. Therefore, if the Communists, or any other modern political leadership, were to create a government capable of succeeding to French rule over all of Vietnam, they clearly would have to adapt their concept of politics to the traditionalist expectations of the Vietnamese peasants.[54]

In their efforts to maintain their influence, the French failed to realize what the Communists came to understand about Vietnamese society and adapted themselves to. Most important of all was the fact that the Vietnamese concept of politics was fashioned over several centuries by the all-powerful action of an intellectual elite whose traditions were adopted from China. The principles and vocabulary of China's history are centered on the idea of a rivalry for power, with Heaven as the arbiter. Its most classical pattern was established during the Chou dynasty, which ended more than two hundred years before the dawn of the Christian era and which witnessed struggles among territorially based feudal states for supremacy over what later became known as central China. As China became more unified under dynastic rule, this competition took the form of feudal groups preparing to become the new dynasty chosen by Heaven to succeed to the supremacy of the dynasty whose "virtue," or political effectiveness, was giving out. This was the game of destiny. The stakes were territorial power, and each person placed his bet on a dynastic faction.

More than any other political movement, the Communists had realized that Vietnam required a modern system of politics if the country was to overcome its long-standing weakness of disunity and foreign rule. But how could any revolutionary leadership adapt itself to the traditional expectations of the peasants, or rather, adapt itself with the effectiveness required to lead the peasants into the modern world, where the politics of mass mobilization and mass participation in political demonstrations and military operations have become the norm? The answer was found in the traditional concept of "virtue," which is the sign that a prevailing regime enjoys the mandate of heaven, enjoys legitimacy in traditionalist terms.[55]

Ho's search for the secret of the strength and the cohesiveness in Vietnam's peasant society, according to McAlister and Mus, was a quest for power to overthrow French rule and make the country united and independent.[56] He found this secret in the peasant's continuing sense of belonging to a larger community beyond the village. By using old, persisting concepts, he created the framework for a new spirit of community based on totally new values. His purpose was to link the villagers to a new sense of Vietnam as a nation by making their traditions relevant to participation in the modern politics of revolution. Instead of the extremely limited participation in politics characteristic of Vietnam's Confucian kingdoms, Ho wanted mass involvement, and to get it he had to persuade villagers to accept new values by linking them to familiar traditions. For Ho, it was a war for the people and not for control over the land. There was no way to turn military force into political authority without creating a bond of community with those in the countryside.

The French never really understood the war; as the Americans would in their turn, they thought of it in terms of terrain controlled, bodies counted. For the French it was a distant war, a war of vanity and pride, whereas to the Vietnamese it was a war of survival—they would pay any price. The French never understood that their absolute military superiority was illusory because Ho and the Vietminh had absolute political superiority. And since this was a political war, it meant that in the long run Ho had the absolute superiority. The French, like the Americans after them, would fight a limited war against a smaller nation that, in contrast, fought *total* war—a war of survival. Time was on Ho's side. Although the French might have won a single battle, battles meant nothing. It was not a war for control of land, but for control of people and their hearts and minds, and in this, Ho was unchallenged.[57]

Shaplen remarks that Ho took the young peasants who had been beaten down by the system and told them that they were as good as the French and the mandarins, that they were as strong and as talented as the upper class, and that, yes, they could rise up.[58] Above all Ho gave the peasant a sense of being a person. Those who had been shown again and again their lack of value now found that they had their rights too—even if only the right to die for an idea, that smallest right. And in doing this Ho finally produced an extraordinary revolutionary force, whose bravery was stunning, and which believed in itself and its cause.

In Graham Greene's *The Quiet American*, when Pyle, the young CIA agent, talked about the Communist's destroying the freedom of the individual, the sour British narrator answered:

But who cared about the individuality of the man in the paddyfield? ... The only man to treat him as a man is the political commissar. He'll sit in his hut and ask his name and listen to his complaints; he'll give up an hour a day to teach him—it doesn't matter what, he's being treated like a man, like someone of value. Don't go on in the East with that parrot cry about a threat to the individual soul. Here you'd find yourself on the wrong side—it's they who stand for the individual, and we just stand for Private 23987, unit in the global strategy."[59]

Ho's strategy was based above all on the population. The army was the people's army; it walked among the people, and it belonged to the people. The orders from Ho were very simple: the army was to work side by side with the population in the fields, help them with their crops, and give them courses in literacy. Above all, the army must honor the population—then and only then would they become one and inseparable, Mao's fish swimming in the water.[60]

Douglas Pike writes about Ho's leadership qualities stating that without Ho Chi Minh the course of Vietnamese history would have been vastly different. He recognized the centrality of image in modern life and at all times projected the correct one—benevolent uncle come to put things right. He maintained a clean background. Much of his success must be credited to his personal qualities, his self-discipline, his asceticism, his selfless dedication, and his immunity (or indifference) to the lures of nepotism, high living, and corruption. Finally, he had a large share of gambler's success, what the world calls luck.[61]

SUMMARY

In summary, I have attempted to explicate three aspects of reconstitutive rhetoric that, before now, have had little or no illumination. The first, and I believe foremost, is the rhetorical power that "character"—developed as a result of "doing," and not through discourse—is a persuasive agent over discourse in the

Vietnamese culture. This character is defined not by the rhetor but, rather, it is defined by cultural heritage. As noted by Charland, Black, Hammerback, and others, Western rhetorical power appears to rest in the discourse rather than the rhetor's character. An interesting example, and perhaps a paradigm, is U.S. public opinion of ex-President Bill Clinton. Embroiled in private scandals, Clinton's character was overwhelmingly dismissed as a necessary and important criterion for leadership by the majority of the general population. In contrast, in Vietnam, it was a person's character, during Ho's time, that was the primary consideration for leadership.

Second, and nearly as important as the first, is the narrow use of the term "collective" by Charland, Black, Hammerback, and others. Their standard and meaning for the word "collective," and the application of that standard, is polar to the Eastern concept of "collective" and its use. Charland and the others assume that "individuality" is the paramount ideology in their understanding of the process of reconstitution. They therefore identify "collectivity" as something that occurs as a result of a "supra" ideological identification, one above and beyond the immediate self. In contrast, in Vietnam, the "collectivity" is the paramount ideology of the immediate self, because the self is philosophically different than the self of the West. "Individuality" is disdained. These differences dramatically influence rhetorical theory and practice, and are only recently being explored by scholars.

The third factor that this text uncovers is the understanding that cultural heritage is and can be used as persuasion. The Confucian concept of revolution, the "Mandate from Heaven," the Sage person, and a worldview perspective are examples of embedded cultural standards for persuasion.

OPPORTUNITY FOR FUTURE STUDY

Archimedes Patti states it best in his summation in *Why Vietnam?*, dated April 1980:

[T]hree decades have passed since events [involving the United States] in Indochina began. In the intervening years the world witnessed the saddest episode in America's history. Castigated and humiliated for its misguided adventurism, the Albatross remains ever present on America's political scene—a scene dominated with an infantile optimism about world capitalist domination that, at best, would isolate the United States and, at worst, precipitate a new world order. It is hardly conceivable that after all that has gone before, our dismal track record in the Far East (China) and Southeast Asia (Vietnam, Cambodia), our national leaders continue to answer the echoes of the past, oblivious to the inevitable consequences.[62]

Tran Van Dinh argues:

Communication research in the Third World has tended to concentrate on the use of modern media by newly independent countries. This ignores the historical communication modes of Third World peoples. Meaningful research should take into account both continuity and revolution because this dialectical Ying-Yang relationship affects both messages and media. Ho Chi Minh, a master of communication, can serve as a good example.[63]

This text explores one mode of Third World communication—that of cultural heritage as rhetorical legacy as a part of reconstitutive discourse—but there are many still to be investigated. A question for further consideration is: Do we, in the West, understand *how* and *why* people in other cultures communicate the way they do, and can this knowledge influence the conflict resolution process prior to committing our nation's resources to armed conflict? The results of such a study would have a lasting impact on how our government officials resolve conflict through communication, improve international relations through understanding, and, most important, preserve that which is most precious—life— by reducing or eliminating unnecessary hostile actions as a result of cultural misunderstanding.

As John Hammerback and Richard Jensen so aptly state, "Whatever the culture of the rhetors and audiences to be examined, scholars in communication studies who seek to discover the rhetorical workings of persuasive messages can profit from considering the rhetorical traditions of ethnic groups whose discourse they study."[64]

NOTES

1. Ho Chi Minh, *Poems from a Prison Diary* (Hanoi: Foreign Languages Publishing House, 1959).

2. John T. McAlister Jr. and Paul Mus, *The Vietnamese and Their Revolution* (New York: Harper and Row, 1970), 21.

3. Jean Lacouture, *Ho Chi Minh: A Political Biography* (New York: Random House, 1968), 101.

4. Jean Chesneaux, *The Vietnamese Nation: Contribution to a History* (Sydney: Current Book Distributors, 1966), 159.

5. Douglas Pike, *History of Vietnamese Communism, 1925–1976* (Stanford, Calif.: Hoover Institution Press, 1978), 52.

6. Chesneaux, *Vietnamese Nation,* 159.

7. Stein Tonnesson, *The Vietnamese Revolution of 1945: Roosevelt, Ho Chi Minh, and de Gaulle in a World at War* (London: Sage, 1991), 389.

8. N. Khac Huyen, *Vision Accomplished? The Enigma of Ho Chi Minh* (New York: Macmillan, 1971), 81.

9. Ibid.

10. Hoang Van Chi, *From Colonialism to Communism: A Case History of North Vietnam* (New York: Frederick A. Praeger, 1964), 60.

11. Tonnesson, *Vietnamese Revolution,* 389.

12. McAlister and Mus, *The Vietnamese and Their Revolution,* 68.

13. Ibid.

14. Ibid., 69.

15. Tonnesson, *Vietnamese Revolution,* 395.

16. McAlister and Mus, *The Vietnamese and Their Revolution,* 60.

17. Ibid., 59.

18. Ibid.

19. Jacques Dalloz, *The War in Indochina, 1945–54* (Dublin: Gill and Macmillan, 1987), 50.

20. Ibid.

21. Ibid., 51.

22. Chesneaux, *Vietnamese Nation*, 161.

23. See William Warby, *Ho Chi Minh and the Struggle for an Independent Vietnam* (London: Merlin, 1972), 3.

24. Tonnesson, *Vietnamese Revolution*, 392.

25. See David Halberstam, *Ho* (New York: Random House, 1971), 70.

26. This is the literal translation of Ho's words. It may be at variance with that of many historians who were not present to hear Ho's delivery, but it is the agreed translation of Vietnamese linguists on Archimedes Patti's staff and that of English-educated Vietnamese translators present on that occasion. See Archimedes Patti, *Why Vietnam? Prelude to America's Albatross* (Berkeley and Los Angeles: University of California Press, 1980), 559.

27. Reinhold Neumann-Hoditz, *Portrait of Ho Chi Minh: An Illustrated Biography*, trans. John Hargreaves (Hamburg: Herder and Herder, 1972), 151. Also see Hue-Tam Ho Tai, *Radicalism and the Origins of the Vietnamese Revolution* (Cambridge: Harvard University Press, 1992), 15.

28. Hy V. Luong, *Revolution in the Village: Tradition and Transformation in North Vietnam, 1925–1988* 131

29. Halberstam, *Ho*, 59–60.

30. Cited in ibid., 60.

31. Ellen Hammer, *Vietnam: Yesterday and Today* (New York: Holt, Rinehart and Winston, 1966), 24.

32. McAlister and Mus, *The Vietnamese and Their Revolution*, 46.

33. Gerald Cannon Hickey, *Village in Vietnam* (New Haven, Conn.: Yale University Press, 1964), 276.

34. Ibid.

35. Ibid.

36. Ibid., 277.

37. Ibid.

38. Ibid.

39. Hue-tam, *Radicalism and the Origins of the Vietnamese Revolution*, 4.

40. Ibid., 4–5.

41. Ibid., 5.

42. Ibid.

43. Ibid., 6–7.

44. Robert Shaplen, *The Lost Revolution* (New York: Harper and Row, 1965), 46.

45. Hue-tam, *Radicalism and the Origins of the Vietnamese Revolution*, 5.

46. Charles Fenn, *Ho Chi Minh: A Biographical Introduction* (New York: Charles Scribner's Sons, 1973), 41.

47. Hue-tam, *Radicalism and the Origins of the Vietnamese Revolution*, 7.

48. Ibid.

49. Ibid., 256.

50. Shaplen, *The Lost Revolution*, 92–93.

51. Shaplen remembers a 1967 interview of a Vietminh colonel who had defected to the American side. He was one of the earliest members of the Vietminh, had risen in rank quickly, and had commanded a battalion. But his father, he said, was something of an itinerant medicine man. Although the son had joined the Vietminh as early as 1945, he spoke with a slightly better accent and dressed a little better than the other soldiers, and he was sure that even though he had excelled in combat, his lack of true peasant origins was being held against him. Perhaps, he said, "If I had been born a peasant, I would be a general now." See Shaplen, *The Lost Revolution*, 93.

52. Hoang, *From Colonialism to Communism*, 60.

53. McAlister and Mus, *The Vietnamese and Their Revolution*, 117.

54. Ibid., 65.

55. Ibid., 113–114.

56. Ibid., 114.

57. Shaplen, *The Lost Revolution*, 96–97.

58. Ibid., 97.

59. Robert Shaplen, *The Lost Revolution* (New York: Harper and Row, 1965), 98.

60. Ibid., 98–99.

61. Pike, *History of Vietnamese Communism*, 60.

62. Patti, *Why Vietnam?*, 448.

63. Tran, V.D., "The Rhetoric of Revolt: Ho Chi Minh as Communicator," *Journal of Communication* 26, no. 4 (Autumn 1976), 147.

64. John C. Hammerback and Richard J. Jensen, "Ethnic Heritage as Rhetorical Legacy: The Plan of Delano," *Quarterly Journal of Speech* 80, no. 1 (February 1994), 67.

Appendix A

Selected Writings of Ho Chi Minh

The eight points that Nguyen Ai Quoc presented to the Versailles Peace Conference were:

1. General amnesty for all Vietnamese political prisoners.
2. Equal rights for Vietnamese and French in Indochina, suppression of the Criminal Commissions which are instruments of terrorism aimed at Vietnamese patriots.
3. Freedom of press and opinion.
4. Freedom of association and assembly.
5. Freedom to travel at home and abroad.
6. Freedom to study and the opening of technical and professional schools for natives of the colonies.
7. Substitute rule of law for government by decree.
8. Appointment of a Vietnamese delegation alongside that of the French government to settle questions relating to Vietnamese interests.[1]

"SPEECH AT THE TOURS CONGRESS"

Chairman: Comrade Indochinese Delegate, you have the floor.

Indochinese Delegate [Nghuyen Ai Quoc]: Today, instead of contributing, together with you, to world revolution, I come here with deep sadness to speak as a member of the Socialist Party, against the imperialists who have committed abhorrent crimes on my native land. You all have known that French imperialism entered Indochina half a century ago. In its selfish interests, it conquered our country with bayonets. Since then we have not only been oppressed and exploited shamelessly, but also tortured and poisoned pitilessly. Plainly speaking, we have been poisoned with opium, alcohol, etc. I cannot, in some minutes, reveal all the atrocities that the predatory capitalists have inflicted on Indochina. Prisons outnumber schools and are always overcrowded with detainees. Any natives having socialist ideas are arrested and sometimes murdered without trial. Such is the so-called justice in Indochina. In that country the Vietnamese are discriminated against, they do not enjoy safety like Europeans or those having European citizenship. We have neither freedom of press nor freedom of speech. Even freedom of assembly and freedom of association do not exist. We have no right to live in other countries or to go abroad as tourists. We are forced to live in utter ignorance and obscurity because we have no right to study. In Indochina the colonialists find all ways and means to force us to smoke opium and drink alcohol to poison and beset us. Thousands of Vietnamese have been led to a slow death or massacred to protect other people's interests.

Comrades, such is the treatment inflicted upon more than 20 million Vietnamese, that is more than half the population of France. And they are said to be under French protection! The Socialist Party must act practically to support the oppressed natives.

Jean Longuet:[2] I have spoken in favor of natives.

Indochinese Delegate: Right from the beginning of my speech I have already asked everyone to keep absolute silence. The Party must make propaganda for socialism in all colonial countries. We have realized that the Socialist Party's joining the Third International means that it has practically promised that from now on it will correctly assess the importance of the colonial question. We are very glad to learn that a Standing Delegation has been appointed to study the North Africa question, and, in the near future, we will be very glad if the Party sends one of its members to Indochina to study on-the-spot the questions relating to this country, and the activities which should be carried out there.

(A right-wing delegate had a contradictory opinion.)

Indochinese Delegate: Silence! You for the Parliament!

Chairman: Now all delegates must keep silence! Including those not standing for the Parliament!

Indochinese Delegate: On behalf of the whole of mankind, on behalf of the Socialist Party's members, both left and right wings, we call upon you! Comrades, save us!

Chairman: Through the applause of approval, the Indochinese Delegate can realize that the whole of the Socialist Party sides with you to oppose the crimes committed by the bourgeois class.[3]

"SOME CONSIDERATIONS ON THE COLONIAL QUESTION"

Since the French Party has accepted Moscow's "twenty-one conditions" and joined the Third International, among the problems which it has set itself is a particularly ticklish one—colonial policy. Unlike the First and Second Internationals, it cannot be satisfied with purely sentimental expressions of position leading to nothing at all, but must have a well-defined working program, an effective and practical policy.

On this point, more than on others, the Party faces many difficulties, the greatest of which are the following:

The Great Size of the Colonies

Not counting the new "trusteeships" acquired after the war, France possesses:
In Asia, 450,000 square kilometers; in Africa, 3,541,000 square kilometers; in America, 108,000 square kilometers; and in Oceana 21,600 square kilometers—a total area of 4,120,000 square kilometers (eight times its own territory), with a population of 48,000,000 souls. These people speak over twenty different languages. This diversity of tongues does not make propaganda easy, for, except in a few old colonies, a French propagandist can make himself understood only through an interpreter. However, translations are of limited value, and in these countries of administrative despotism, it is rather difficult to find an interpreter to translate revolutionary speeches.

There are other drawbacks: Though the natives of all the colonies are equally oppressed and exploited, their intellectual, economic, and political development differs greatly from one region to another. Between Annam and the Congo, Martinique and New Caledonia, there is absolutely nothing in common, except poverty.

The Indifference of the Proletariat of the Mother Country Toward the Colonies

In his theses on the colonial question, Lenin clearly stated that "the workers of colonizing countries are bound to give the most active assistance to the liberation movements in subject countries." To this end, the workers of the mother country must know what a colony really is, they must be acquainted with what is going on there, and with the suffering—a thousand times more acute than theirs—endured by their brothers, the proletarians in the colonies. In a word, they must take an interest in this question.

Unfortunately, there are many militants who still think that a colony is nothing but a country with plenty of sand underfoot and of sun overhead, a few green coconut palms and colored folk, that is all. And they take not the slightest interest in the matter.

The Ignorance of the Natives

In colonized countries—in old Indochina as well as in new Dahomey—the class struggle and proletarian strength are unknown factors for the simple reason that there are neither big commercial and industrial enterprises nor workers' organizations. In the eyes of the natives, Bolshevism—a word which is the more vivid and expressive because frequently used by the bourgeoisie—means either the destruction of everything or emancipation from the foreign yoke. The first sense given to the word drives the ignorant and timorous masses away from us; the second leads them to nationalism. Both senses are equally dangerous. Only a tiny section of the intelligentsia knows what is meant by Communism. But these gentry, belonging to the native bourgeoisie and supporting the bourgeois colonialists, have no interest in the Communist doctrine being understood and propagated. On the contrary, like the dog in the fable, they prefer to bear the mark of the collar and to have their piece of bone. Generally speaking, the masses are thoroughly rebellious, but completely ignorant. They want to free themselves, but do not know how to go about doing so.

Prejudices

The mutual ignorance of the two proletariats gives rise to prejudices. The French workers look upon the native as an inferior and negligible human being, incapable of understanding and still less of taking action. The natives regard all the French as wicked exploiters. Imperialism and capitalism do not fail to take advantage of this mutual suspicion and this artificial racial hierarchy to frustrate propaganda and divide forces which ought to unite.

Fierceness of Repression

If the French colonialists are unskillful in developing colonial resources, they are masters in the art of savage repression and the manufacture of loyalty made to measure. The Gandhis and the DeValeras would have long since entered heaven had they been born in one of the French colonies. Surrounded by all the refinements of courts martial and special courts, a native militant cannot educate his oppressed and ignorant brothers without the risk of falling into the clutches of his civilizers.

Faced with these difficulties, what must the Party do?

Intensify propaganda to overcome them.

"RACIAL HATRED"

For having spoken of the class struggle and equality among men, and on the charge of having preached racial hatred, our comrade Louzon[4] has been sentenced.

Let us see how the love between peoples has been understood and applied in Indochina of late. We will not speak for the time being of the poisoning and degradation of the masses by alcohol and opium of which the colonial government is guilty; our comrades in the parliamentary group will have to deal with this matter one day.

Everybody knows the deeds of derring-do of the assassin-administrator Darles. However, he is far from having the monopoly of savagery against the natives.

A certain Pourcignon furiously rushed upon an Annamese who was so curious and bold as to look at this European's house for a few seconds. He beat him and finally shot him down with a bullet in the head.

A railway official beat a Tonkinese village mayor with a cane. M. Beck broke his driver's skull with a blow from his fist. M. Bres, building contractor, kicked an Annamese to death after binding his arms and letting him be bitten by his dog. M. Deffis, receiver, killed his Annamese servant with a powerful kick in the kidneys.

M. Henry, a mechanic at Haiphong, heard a noise in the street; the door of his house opened, (an) Annamese woman came in, pursued by a man. Henry, thinking that it was a native chasing after a *con-gai*,[5] snatched up his hunting rifle and shot him. The man fell, stone dead: It was a European. Questioned, Henry replied, "I thought it was a native."

A Frenchman lodged his horse in a stable in which there was a mare belonging to a native. The horse pranced, throwing the Frenchman into a furious rage. He beat the native, who began to bleed from the mouth and ears, after which he bound his hands and hung him from them under his staircase.

A missionary (oh yes, a gentle apostle!), suspecting a native seminarist of having stolen 1,000 piasters from him, suspended him from a beam and beat him. The poor fellow lost consciousness. He was taken down. When he came to, it began again. He was dying, and is perhaps dead already.…

Has justice punished these individuals, these civilizers? Some have been acquitted and others were not troubled by the law at all. That's that.

And now, accused Louzon, it's your turn to speak!

"ANNAMESE WOMEN AND FRENCH DOMINATION"

Colonization is in itself an act of violence of the stronger against the weaker. This violence becomes still more odious when it is exercised upon women and children.

It is bitterly ironic to find that civilization—symbolized in its various forms, *viz.*, liberty, justice, etc., by the gentle image of a woman, and run by a category of men well known to be champions of gallantry—inflicts on its living emblem the most ignoble treatment and afflicts her shamefully in her manners, her modesty, and even her life.

Colonial sadism is unbelievably widespread and cruel, but we shall confine ourselves here to recalling a few instances seen and described by witnesses unsuspected of partiality. These facts will allow our Western sisters to realize both the nature of the "civilizing mission" of capitalism, and the sufferings of their sisters in the colonies.

"On the arrival of the soldiers," relates a colonial, "the population fled; there only remained two old men and two women: one maiden, and a mother suckling her baby and holding an eight-year-old girl by the hand. The soldiers asked for money, spirits, and opium.

"As they could not make themselves understood, they became furious and knocked down one of the old men with their rifle butts. Later, two of them, already drunk when they arrived, amused themselves for many hours by roasting the other old man at a wood fire. Meanwhile, the others raped the two women and the eight-year-old girl. Then, weary, they murdered the girl. The mother was then able to escape with her infant and, from a hundred yards off, hidden in a bush, she saw her companion tortured. She did not know why the murder was perpetrated, but she saw the young girl lying on her back, bound and gagged, and one of the men, many times, slowly thrust his bayonet into her stomach and, very slowly, draw it out again. Then he cut off the dead girl's finger to take a ring, and her head to steal a necklace.

"The three corpses lay flat on the ground of a former salt-marsh: the eight-year-old girl naked, the young woman disemboweled, her stiffened left forearm raising a clenched fist to the indifferent sky, and the old man, horrible, naked like the others, disfigured by the roasting with his fat which had run, melted, and congealed with the skin of his belly, which was bloated, grilled, and golden, like the skin of a roast pig."

"AN OPEN LETTER TO M. ALBERT SARRAUT, MINISTER OF COLONIES"

Your Excellency,

We know very well that your affection for the natives of the colonies in general, and the Annamese in particular, is great.

Under your proconsulate the Annamese people have known true prosperity and real happiness, the happiness of seeing their country dotted all over with an increasing number of spirit and opium shops which, together with firing squads, prisons, "democracy," and all the improved apparatus of modern civilization, are combining to make the Annamese the most advanced of the Asians and the happiest of mortals.

These acts of benevolence (save) us the trouble of recalling all the others, such as recruitment and loans, bloody repressions, the dethronement and exile of kings, profanation of sacred places, etc.

As a Chinese poem says, "The wind of kindness follows the movement of your fan, and the rain of virtue precedes the tracks of your carriage." As you are now the supreme head of all the colonies, your special care for the Indochinese has but increased with your elevation. You have created in Paris itself a service having the special task—with special regard to Indochina, according to a colonial publication—of keeping watch on the natives, especially the Annamese, living in France.

But "keeping watch" alone seemed to Your Excellency's fatherly solicitude insufficient, and you wanted to do better. That is why for some time now, you have granted each Annamese—dear Annamese, as Your Excellency says—private *aides-de-camp*. Though still novices in the art of Sherlock Holmes, these good people are very devoted and particularly sympathetic. We have only praise to bestow on them and compliments to pay their boss, Your Excellency.

We are sincerely moved by the honor that Your Excellency has the extreme kindness to grant us and we should have accepted it with all gratitude if it did not seem a little superfluous and if it did not excite envy and jealousy.

At a time when Parliament is trying to save money and cut down administrative personnel, when there is large budget deficit, when agriculture and industry lack labor, when attempts are being made to levy taxes on workers' wages, and at a time when repopulation demands the use of all productive energies, it would seem to us antipatriotic at such a time to accept personal favors which necessarily cause loss of the powers of the citizens condemned—as *aides-de-camp*—to idleness and the spending of money that the proletariat has sweated hard for.

In consequence, while remaining obliged to you, we respectfully decline this distinction flattering to us but too expensive to the country.

If Your Excellency insists on knowing what we do every day, nothing is easier: We shall publish every morning a bulletin of our movements, and Your Excellency will have but the trouble of reading.

Besides, our timetable is quite simple and almost unchanging.

Morning: from 8 to 12 at the workshop.

Afternoon: in newspaper offices (leftist, of course) or at the library.

Evening: at home or attending educational talks.

Sundays and holidays: visiting museums or other places of interest.

There you are!

Hoping that this convenient and rational method will give satisfaction to Your Excellency, we beg to remain....

Nguyen Ai Quoc

"AN OPEN LETTER TO M. LEON ARCHIMBAUD"

Sir,

In your speech to the Chamber of Deputies you said that if you had wished to do so, you could have denounced colonial scandals, but you prefer to pass over in silence the crimes and offenses committed by your civilizers in the colonies. This is your right and it concerns only you, your conscience, and your electors. As for us who have suffered and will continue to suffer every day from these "blessings" of colonialism, we do not need you to tell us about them.

But when, writing in *Le Rappel*, you say that the facts pointed out by citizen Bourneton[6] are false or exaggerated, you yourself "exaggerate!" First, the Minister of Colonies himself was obliged to recognize that a "contemptuous state of mind toward native life" exists. And that he "denied no act of brutality" denounced by Deputy Boisneuf. And then can you deny, M. Archimbaud, that during the last few years, that is to say, following the war for "the rule of law" for which 800,000 natives came to work "voluntarily" or to be killed in France, that your civilizers—with impunity—have robbed, swindled, murdered, or burnt alive Annamese, Tunisians, and Senegalese?

You write next that the acts of injustice are more numerous in France than in the colonies. Then allow me to tell you, M. Archimbaud, that one should not pretend to give lessons in equality or justice to others when one is unable to apply them at home. This is the most elementary logic, isn't it?

According to you, the doings of your colonial administrators are known, commented upon, and controlled by the Governments General and the Ministry of Colonies. Hence it must be one of two things. Either you are harebrained and have forgotten the Baudoins, the Darles, the Lucases, and so many others making up the galaxy which is the honor and pride of your Colonial Administration, and who, after having committed heinous crimes, receive as punishment only promotions and decorations. Or else you are treating your readers as complete fools.

You state that if France has sinned in colonial matters it is rather from an excess of generous sentiment than anything else. Will you tell us, M. Archimbaud, whether it is out of these generous sentiments that the natives are deprived of all rights to write, speak, and travel, etc.? Is it out of these same sentiments that the ignoble condition of "native" is imposed on them, that they are robbed of their land only to see it given to the conquerors, and forced thereafter to work as slaves? You yourselves have said that the Tahitian race has been decimated by alcoholism and is disappearing. Is it also from an excess of generosity that you are doing all you can to intoxicate the Annamese with your alcohol and stupefy them with your opium?

You speak finally of "duty," "humanity," and "civilization"! What is this duty? You showed what it is throughout your speech. It is markets, competition, interests, privileges. Trade and finance are things which express your "humanity." Taxes, forced labor, excessive exploitation, that is the summing up of your civilization!

While you are waiting to receive "one of the finest claims to glory that can be dreamt of," allow me to tell you, M. Archimbaud, that if Victor Hugo had known that you would write such stuff today in his newspaper, he would never have founded it.

Respectfully yours,

Nguyen Ai Quoc

"ANNAMESE PEASANT CONDITIONS"

The Annamese in general are crushed by the blessings of French protection. The Annamese peasants especially are still more odiously crushed by this protection: as Annamese they are oppressed; as peasants they are robbed, plundered, expropriated, and ruined. It is they who do all the hard labor, all the *corvees*. It is they who produce for the whole horde of parasites, loungers, civilizers, and others. And it is they who live in poverty while their executioners live in plenty and who die of starvation when their crops fail. This is due to the fact that they are robbed on all sides and in all ways by the Administration, by modern feudalism, and by the Church. In former times, under the Annamese regime, lands were classified into several categories according to their capacity for production. Taxes were based on this classification. Under the present colonial regime, all this has changed. When money is wanted, the French Administration simply has the categories modified. With a stroke of their magic pen, they have transformed poor land into fertile land, and the Annamese peasant is obliged to pay more in taxes on his fields than they can yield him.

That is not all. Areas are artificially increased by reducing the unit of measure. As a result, taxes are automatically increased by a third in some localities, by two-thirds in others. Yet this is not sufficient to appease the voracity of the protector State, which increases the taxes year by year. Thus, from 1890 to 1896, taxes doubled. They were further increased by a half from 1896 to 1898, and so on. The Annamese continued to let themselves be fleeced, and our "protectors," encouraged by the success of these operations, continued their spoliation.

Often despotism was mixed with plunder. In 1895, for example, the Administrator of a province in Tonkin stripped a village of several hectares to the advantage of another village, the latter a Catholic one. The plundered peasants lodged a complaint. They were jailed. Don't think that administrative cynicism stopped there. The unfortunates who had been robbed were obliged to pay taxes until 1910 on lands which had been taken away from them in 1895!

On the heels of a thieving Administration came the thieving settlers. Europeans, who, for all their ideas of agriculture and farming skill, possessed only a big belly and a white skin, were given concessions whose size often surpassed 20,000 hectares.

Most of these concessions were founded on legalized theft. During the course of the conquest, the Annamese peasants, like the Alsatians in 1870, had abandoned their lands to seek refuge in the still free part of the country. When they came back, their lands had been given away. Entire villages were thus plundered, and the natives reduced to tenants of the lords of a modern feudalism, who sometimes appropriated as much as 90 percent of the crops.

On the pretext of encouraging colonization, exemption from land taxes was made in favor of a great number of these big landholders.

After securing the land at no cost whatsoever, the landholders obtained manpower for nothing or next to nothing. The Administration supplied them with numbers of convicts who worked for nothing, or used its machinery to recruit workers for them who were paid starvation wages. If the Annamese did not come in sufficient numbers or if they showed discontent, violence was then resorted to: Landholders seized the mayors and notables of villages, cudgeled and tortured them until these unfortunates had signed a contract pledging themselves to supply the required number of workers.

Besides this temporal power, there are spiritual "saviors" who, while preaching the virtue of poverty to the Annamese, are no less zealous in seeking to enrich themselves through the sweat and blood of the natives. In Cochinchina alone, the "Sainte Mission Apostolique" on its own possesses one-fifth of the ricefields in the region. Though not taught in the Bible, the method of obtaining these lands was very simple: usury and corruption. The Mission took advantage of the years when crops failed to lend money to peasants, obliging them to pawn their lands as a guarantee. The rate of interest was usurious, and the Annamese could not pay off their debts at the due time; as a result, all pledged lands fell into the possession of the Mission. The more or less generous governors to whom the mother country entrusted the destiny of Indochina were generally dolts or blackguards. It was enough for the Mission to have in its hands certain secret, personal, and compromising papers to be able to frighten them and obtain from them whatever it wanted. In this way, one Governor General conceded to the Mission 7,000 hectares of river land belonging to natives, who were thus at one stroke reduced to beggary.

From this brief survey, one can see that behind a mask of democracy, French imperialism has transplanted in Annam the whole cursed medieval regime, including the salt tax, and that the Annamese peasant is crucified on the bayonet of capitalist civilization and on the Cross of prostituted Christianity.

"DUONG KACH MENH" (REVOLUTIONARY ROAD)

What is the primary requisite for revolution?

First, it is necessary to have a revolutionary party which, internally, can motivate and organize the masses and which, externally, can contact oppressed peoples and the proletarian class everywhere. A strong revolutionary party is a prerequisite to success just as a strong helmsman is a strong prerequisite to the operation of a boat.

In order to have a strong party, it must have an ideology. Everyone in the party must understand that ideology and everyone must obey it. A party without an ideology is like a person without intelligence or a boat without a compass.

We are studying a lot of theory and ideology now but the most genuine, most correct, and most revolutionary ideology is Leninism.

"AFTER PRISON, A WALK IN THE MOUNTAINS"

> The clouds embrace the peaks,
> the peaks embrace the clouds,
> The river below shines like a mirror,
> spotless and clean.
> On the crest of the Western Mountains,
> my heart stirs as I wander
> Looking toward the Southern sky
> and dreaming of old friends.

NOTES

1. The selection of writings of Ho Chi Minh in this appendix are presented in their entirety. Please note that these writings have been reproduced by various persons and agencies and that the reproductions I have viewed are not exact; that is, word(s) or even

entire phrases have been either changed or omitted. The writings offered in this text are reproductions of the originals and have not been edited and can be viewed at Texas Tech University, Center for the Study of the Vietnam Conflict, Lubbock, Texas.

2. A leader of the orthodox Socialist wing of the party, and a nephew of Karl Marx.

3. Nguyen Ai Quoc, "Speech at the Tours Congress," *Writings of Ho Chi Minh*, Indochina Archives, University of California, Berkeley, located in DRV file, Subj BIOG, Date December 1920, Sub-cat Ho Chi Minh. Also see Jean Lacouture, *Ho Chi Minh: A Political Biography* (New York: Random House, 1968), 27–28.

4. A native of a French colony; a French Communist persecuted by the colonists.

5. Vietnamese for "young girl"; used by the French colonialists to mean a native mistress of a Frenchman.

6. A member of Parliament, representative of the French Communist Party.

Appendix B

Reliable Sources: A Bibliographic Essay

A comprehensive search of the literature on the reconstitutive rhetoric of Ho Chi Minh confirmed my initial belief that no academic studies have been undertaken in this area. I did find numerous biographical studies on the life and times of Ho Chi Minh, research studies on the history and development of the Vietnamese culture, and countless books on the Indochinese war. However, many were not considered to be reliable sources because of historical inaccuracies, unsubstantiated quotations, and the inclusion of nonverifiable occurrences. As for the extants attributed to Ho Chi Minh and translated into English, I relied on the expertise of Douglas Pike.[1] English translations of Chinese texts, for the purpose of fleshing out classical Chinese philosophy, were verified by Professor Ho Ting Hui and Professor Jensen Chung.[2] For the purpose of this text, the literature chosen as reliable sources is presented in four categories: the political culture of Vietnam; philosophical foundations of the Vietnamese worldview; biography of Ho Chi Minh's thought and character; and selected extant writings, poems, and speeches of Ho Chi Minh. It must be noted that some sources are cited in more than one area because of their relevance.[3]

Origins of Vietnamese Politics

For this section I have chosen twelve reliable and respected authors and their works. They are Paul Mus, John McAlister Jr., Douglas Pike, Ellen Hammer, William Duiker, Stein Tonnesson, Jacques Dalloz, Jean Chesneaux, John DeFrancis, David Marr, Hue-Tam Ho Tai, and Ralph Smith.

Perhaps the most knowledgeable individual to record Vietnamese political culture was Professor Paul Mus.[4] John McAlister Jr. coauthored the first text with Mus, and shortly after Mus' death wrote a second text.[5] McAlister and Mus concluded that the conflict in Vietnam could best be understood as a revolution, "perhaps not in the classic sense of revolution in France and Russia, but as a series of changes so convulsive and pervasive as to call into question conventional conceptions of revolution." As a part of their assessment of that conflict they stated, "The fact that Asian revolutions and, in particular, revolution in Vietnam do not conform to prevailing concepts of revolutionary politics is undoubtedly a part of our problem of adapting our perceptions and policies to the situation as it exists."[6]

McAlister and Mus' analysis was comprehensive and concluded that one must understand the Vietnamese concept of revolution before one can understand Vietnamese politics. Their initial study focuses on four critical areas of the historical structure of Vietnamese revolution and its relevance to Vietnamese culture. The first of these details Vietnam's tradition of political disunity; the second traces the history of French rule in Vietnam; the third study investigates the colonial background to the Vietnamese revolution (1885–1940; which include the transformation of Vietnamese politics and society and the genesis of Vietnamese nationalism); and the fourth focuses on the wartime impact on revolutionary politics: the Japanese occupation of Indochina (1940–1945). Their second study[7] focuses on comparing traditional Vietnamese concepts of revolution and political community (which include the political power of the Vietnamese peasant, concepts of individual responsibility, the village foundation of Vietnamese society, and the Vietnamese model of China's social system) to the politics of modernization: Marxism.

Douglas Pike's historiography of Communism in Vietnam is critical for understanding Vietnamese political dynamics.[8] This study offers five major areas of consideration: the birth of Vietnamese Communism; the challenges and frustrations of the Communist Party in the 1930s; the opportunity for the Communists as a result of World War II; leadership in the name of Ho Chi Minh; and the crucible years of the Viet Minh War.

William Duiker's first text on the Vietnamese revolution focuses on two historical aspects important for this dissertation.[9] The first fleshes out those who became revolutionaries—the scholar–patriots and the urban nationalists; the second explicates the political constructs of the social revolutionaries, which include the Revolutionary Youth League and the red Soviets of Nghe-Tinh.

Duiker's second text on the Vietnamese revolution contains three major areas of importance to this text.[10] The first focuses on the roots of revolution, which includes the nature of French colonialism, sources of nationalism and communism, the coming of World War II, and the August Revolution. The second addresses Vietnamese politics and government. Here the focus is on the dynamics of Vietnamese political tradition, the impact of the West, the Marxist alternative, and the role of the Communist Party as a leading force in the Vietnamese revolution. The third major area of importance illuminates culture and society: philosophy and religion, education in Confucian Vietnam, culture and ideology, and the evolution of Vietnamese culture in contemporary Marxist perspective.

Ellen Hammer wrote, "The assumptions of Western political analysis do not offer much guidance within the Vietnamese context."[11] Her study offers an in-depth analysis of two major topics important to this text. The first focuses on philosophy and religion, including Confucianism, Taoism, Buddhism, Catholicism, and the numerous politico–religious sects. The second offers a comprehensive assessment of Vietnamese social institutions: the family and village. She found that the Vietnamese system of government, influenced by its numerous religions, bore little similarity to governmental systems of the West. Also, the Vietnamese social institutions of the family and village were conceptually dissimilar to those of the West.

Stein Tonnesson offers a historiographical sketch focused exclusively on the Vietnamese revolution.[12] I have not been able to locate a superior and more comprehensive analysis of the political events that led to Ho Chi Minh's pronouncement of the declaration of Vietnamese independence on 2 September 1945.

Focusing on the colonial Indochinese period, Jacques Dalloz performs an extensive analysis beginning with Napoleon III's conquest and the sociopolitical changes that resulted from French colonialism to French disgrace at Dien Bien Phu in 1954.[13] His assessment of the cataclysmic changes to the Vietnamese religious culture and political system from the period 1885–1945 is of extreme importance. Dalloz painstakingly explains the metamorphic change from traditional philosophical, political, and moral systems to those of French modernity.

Jean Chesneaux studied the revolutionary period between 1922 and 1946.[14] He explains how the French attempted to dismember and replace the Vietnamese political system with its own political system. The major foci relevant to this text are: the end of Vietnamese independence and the setting up of the colonial machinery (1882–1905); Vietnam under the colonial system (1905–1930): new forms of the national movement, economic dependence, and social disorder; and world crisis and world war: bankruptcy of the colonial system in Vietnam (1930–1945).

John DeFrancis has approached his research into Vietnam and the era of French colonialism from a unique perspective—that of the sociolinguistic aspects of language.[15] His historiography explicates the changes in the Vietnamese language from classical Chinese to Quoc Ngu and the failed attempt by the French to eliminate Quoc Ngu and replace it with French as the official national language. DeFrancis has captured not only resulting cultural changes, but also changes in the political and philosophical structures that fueled nationalism.

Hue-Ho Tai's study of the Vietnamese revolution is unique, to say the least, for it comes to us from a scholar's perspective.[16] Hue-Tam focuses on the role of radicalism in the early phase of the Vietnamese Revolution and its eventual displacement by Marxism–Leninism as the dominant force in reshaping anticolonial politics and as the source of language for discussing cultural, social, and political issues.

David Marr's first study centers on certain political events at the turn of the century in Vietnam.[17] He focuses on the reasons the Communists were successful in Vietnam and the non-Communists were not. This historiographical approach is almost entirely of the Indochinese Communist Party, the Vietminh, and the National Liberation Front (more properly known as the National Front for Liberation of South Vietnam).

Marr's second study explores the Vietnamese scholar gentry.[18] He focuses on the relationship between ethics and politics, and with problems of social harmony and social struggle as they relate to theory and practice and how this all became a part of organized political movements.

Ralph Smith's essay focuses on Vietnam's tragic relationship with the West.[19] He looked at the period from 1858 to 1963, slightly over a century, in which Vietnam moved from the last days of monarchical independence, on the eve of French conquest, to a situation of divided independence in which the two halves (North and South) of the country were at war with one another. Smith states that by the time Vietnam became independent (1945) the traditional Vietnamese political system was dead. He explains that there was no inherent reason why Communism was more appropriate to Vietnam's needs than a system incorporating Western ideas about government and economic growth.[1] He attributes much of Communism's success to Ho Chi Minh.

Origins of Vietnamese Philosophy and Religion

This area of study illuminates traditional philosophy and religion adopted by the Vietnamese. For this section, I rely on the works of Wm. Theodore de Bary, David Hall and Roger Ames, Herrlee Creel, E.R. Hughes, Miles Meander Dawson, Lin Yutang, Mary Garrett, and Xing Lu and David A. Frank.

Wm. Theodore de Bary offers a historiography of China, from the Classical Period to Mao Tse Tung.[20] However, the areas of de Bary's study that are relevant to this text begin with the Classical Period, which includes the Chinese tradition in antiquity (*I ching* [Book of Changes], *Shu ching* [Book of History], *Shih ching* [Book of Odes], *Li chi* [Book of Rites], and the *Ch'un ch'iu* [Spring and Autumn Annals]). Next is the study of *K'ung Fu-tzu* (Confucius) and the impact that Confucianism had on traditional Vietnamese society; followed by the metaphysics and government of *Lao tzu* or Tao-te Ching, and its influence on the people; the important roles that the *Imperial Order* (the theoretical basis of the Imperial institution, the moral leadership of the emperor, the theory of Portents, and the Dynastic Mandate) played on the creation and maintenance of the Vietnamese traditional political system. The last area focuses on the Universal Order. This includes the creation of the universe, theories of the structure of the universe, the "Great Appendix" to the *Book of Changes*, the process of universal change, and the beginning of human culture.

Two critical areas of importance to this study are explicated by David Hall and Roger Ames.[21] The first fleshes out the differences between the philosophic ancient Chinese culture and the philosophic Western culture. And the second illuminates the principles of Confucius from a Chinese perspective.

Ames' historiographical analysis of classical China underscores the philosophical importance of Sun-tzu from the cultural perspective, whereas most scholars have approached the study of Sun-tzu from a historical perspective.[22] Ames explains the intimate relationship between philosophy and warfare. Within this analysis, he discusses assumptions about the classical Chinese world-view, classical Western worldview, centripetal harmony and authority, warfare as an *art* of contextualizing, the strategic advantage, and the exemplary commander.

Herrlee Creel studied the development of the Western Chou Empire.[23] His explication of the origin, development, and enduring implications of the "Mandate of Heaven" is significant for this study. Included in this study is Creel's understanding of the *organizational process* of the royal government.

In this source, "Chinese Thought from Confucius to Mao Tse-tung," Creel focuses mainly on the history of Chinese thought before the beginning of the Christian Era.[24] Factors that influenced Vietnamese culture include the Chinese view before Confucius, Confucius and the struggle for human happiness, Mencius and the emphasis on human nature, the mystical skepticism of the Taoists, and the effects of Buddhism and Neo-Confucianism.

From Creel's "Sinism: A Study of the Evolution of the Chinese World-View," his description of the origins and development of Chinese thought, from the earliest period about which we can reasonably speculate through the period of the classical philosophical systems, are the corpus of this text.[25] Creel features some of the most important developments in Chinese philosophy and religion, emphasizing classical philosophers and their ideas in relation to mainstream Chinese thought.

The importance of Creel's discussion of Confucius lies in his biographical assessments of the man and the influences of Confucianism on China and on Western democracy.[26] Of importance to this study are the assumptions made about Confucius the man and the philosopher and the eventual influences that Confucianism had on western Europe and democracy when introduced by returning missionaries.

E.R. Hughes' work illuminates the new powers of reasoning that emerged in classical Chinese thought.[27] These powers include three very important developments: Confucius and the discovery of the self-conscious moral individual; the philosophical mind of Tzu Ssu and his search for reality; and *Mo Ti*, the rise of religious utilitarianism and the cultivation of the moral self.

Miles Meander Dawson offers an extensive and in-depth analysis of Confucius and his teachings.[28] He begins with Confucius' assumptions about what constitutes the "superior man," including the *art* of living; mental morality; the investigation of phenomena; learning, genius, and inspiration; sincerity; rectification of purpose; and rectified purpose. Dawson next investigates the Confucian concept of *self-development:* the will, fortitude, poise, self-control, moderation, righteousness, earnestness, humility, aspiration, and prudence. From self-development the notion of *general human relations* is fleshed out: the rules of propriety, propriety of *demeanor*, propriety of *deportment*, propriety of *speech*, propriety of *conduct*, and propriety of *example*. From the

Confucian position on family, essentials of *filial piety* is of most importance to this study. The *state* follows the family. Focus on the foundation of government, the function of government, the idea that government exists for the *benefit* of the governed, the essentials of good government, the nourishment of the people, the middle path in political economy, *kingly* qualities, power of *official example*, universal education, government is by the *consent* of the governed, and the crucial dictum—"the right to *depose* the ruler"—are all critical factors influencing Vietnamese politics. Dawson completes his investigation with *universal relations*, the Confucian belief in death and immortality, spiritual beings and spiritual power, *Heaven*, providence, and *God*.

Lin Yutang focuses solely on the wisdom of Confucius.[29] Two areas necessary for understanding Vietnamese thought are the Confucian concepts of *central harmony* and *ethics and politics*, which Yutang painstakingly describes.

Two journal articles of import address classical Chinese rhetorical theories. The first, by Mary Garrett, focuses on the rhetorical background of the classical period, also known as the "Warring States Period," the psychological principles that apply both to the mass and single-person audiences, moving the "heart of the one-person audience," and explores the implications of *pathos* in these contexts.[30] The second, by Xing Lu and David Frank, focuses on the study of Chinese rhetoric from a non-Occidental tradition.[31] They analyze modes of inquiry from both Chinese and Western perspectives and delineate their conclusions and implications about the study of Chinese *bian* and the rhetoric of other traditions.

Biography of Ho Chi Minh

This area of study focuses on the bibliographical accounts of Ho Chi Minh. Here I have chosen Archimedes Patti, who offers a firsthand account of the earliest military presence of the United States in Indochina, beginning with the year 1942 and progressing rapidly to the critical year 1945.[32] Of particular interest is Patti's presentation of events (chronologically recorded) as they occurred and his experiences in China and Vietnam with the French, Chinese, and Vietnamese, including his first meeting with Ho Chi Minh. Patti also describes his numerous encounters with Ho—Ho's demeanor and character—while advising him during World War II, and as he assisted Ho in drafting the Vietnamese Declaration of Independence.

METHOD FOR HISTORICAL ANALYSIS

I have chosen a specific means with which to analyze materials relevant to this study. It is called a historical–critical method, which enables an in-depth examination of a past event—the Vietnamese revolution for independence from French colonialism—and the ability for the reader to draw conclusions from it. The applicability of the method for this type of research is explained by Raymond K. Tucker, Richard L. Weaver, and Cynthia Berryman-Fink as:

Many fields and professionals realize that historical study is indispensable to their own proficiency. Thus, a familiarity with historical methodology broadens our professional base. And as we acquire this professional training, we are also likely to acquire the values that result from a study of the past: perspective, understanding, tolerance, and appreciation.... . Too often we think of historical research as that which is intended to discover and describe past events. That is a narrow view. A more contemporary view is that historical research provides a perspective for the interpretation of the present, understanding present facts, customs, traditions, trends, and movements. Characteristics of present society can be traced to the past.[33]

Every problem has its roots in the past. Tucker, Weaver, and Berryman-Fink state: "Whether history is the central focus or simply incidental to a study, every speech-communication scholar should know how to study the past."[34] However, historical–critical methods do not stop with a description of what has been. Tucker, Weaver, and Berryman-Fink conclude: "They must also suggest interpretation of the past to serve three important purposes: (1) to show why things developed as they did; (2) to show how they compared with other similar developments; and (3) to indicate a judgment of worth—how effective or ineffective, good or bad, or right or wrong."[35]

This historical analysis examines the *movement/idea* of Ho Chi Minh's quest for an independent Vietnam. Tucker, Weaver, Berryman-Fink suggest that:

Such studies cover a wide variety of topics: factors that give rise to movements; conditions under which leaders emerge and followers are welded together; roles played by authorities; stages through which movements develop; comparative merits of alternative modes of influence for achieving different goals; varied consequences of movement activity; and varied fates of movements.[36]

Central within the *movement/idea* is the perception of *character* and the audience's identification with that character. In the Sino/Vietnamese tradition, character is paramount. For Ho, character was, arguably, *the* most important factor in his successful campaign. Frederick Antczak states:

Appealing to an audience preoccupied with the relation of character and authority, it used the speaker's distinctive virtues to represent his kind of thought as an actually truer, richer, more authoritative fulfillment of the audience's own essential character. The virtues that the specialty brings were of course represented as the audience's own virtues—only in an advanced, advantaged state, far more complete and compelling.[37]

Antczak explicates the connection between identification and character with:

Thus the educator also "represented" his audience—represented the achievable best in his audience. He represented what his audience could become if they were educated to the deepest meanings and richest possibilities of their identity. Since "what we admire, we learn to imitate," the speaker's admirable virtues evoked from listeners the wish to emulate the ethical principles that made him admirable, all in order to become more like the speaker and thus paradoxically more like themselves—for he was like them, only more so.[38]

The introduction of Marxism–Leninism into Vietnamese politics by Ho Chi Minh and subsequent acceptance by the Vietnamese people can best be explained by Antczak: He states that "the virtues of the speaker's character were directly related to the principles of the special kind of thought that he was expounding," and that "[t]hrough a rhetoric of representation and identification, thought and character could be brought into an ethically authoritative relation for the ... audience."[39]

Subsumed within Tucker, Weaver, and Berryman-Fink's *movement/idea*, Western "thought," a primary element of reconstitutive rhetoric, is used as a comparable foundation to the Vietnamese rhetorical process and its philosophical influences. Richard Cherwitz argues that "all serious inquiries are at root philosophical," and that the "fundamental questions raised by rhetoricians have been and will always be about the world of prudential conduct."[40] James Hikins supports this, adding that "the understanding of realism is of utmost importance for the rhetorical theorist because rhetorical practice is ensconced in the pedestrian world, and because its most direct consequences bear on issues of human conduct and welfare, any theory of rhetoric must eventually land squarely on its feet *in* the pedestrian world."[41] Barry Brummett concludes with the statement that, "the belief that what is real and true is determined only by the social, symbolic, and historical context from which the knowing human arises."[42]

Another aspect for understanding Ho's rhetoric, that of language, is articulated by Joaquin Barcelo. He states that "the communication we establish through language is the transfer to our fellowmen of our particular experience in reality," and that "[l]anguage is not universal. Every epoch and every people, and even every individual have peculiar shades of language."[43] According to Barcelo, language is not univocal or unambiguous; it is essentially equivocal, vague, and misleading. He claims that there is yet something that is even more problematic, that permanently deepens the crisis of language and communication. He states that "[l]anguage allows us to express a certain experience of reality, but this experience is brought about or awakened by real objects we face, and these objects, even the most concrete, do not have a universal meaning either."[44] An example: Ba Dinh Square in Hanoi is a completely different reality to the old lady who lives in its neighborhood, and who witnessed Ho Chi Minh declare Vietnamese independence in 1945; to the French army that fought the Vietminh in Ba Dinh Square; or the American advisers who were present during Ho's declaration of independence. Nonetheless, language only says "Ba Dinh Square," seemingly forgetful of the diversity of these possible multiple experiences, but in fact including them all. Language, like the oracle at Delphi, shows through concealing.

Mary Garrett says that sinologists have devoted much attention to the types of arguments that predominate in Chinese discourse. They generally agree that the preferred modes of argumentation used by the classical Chinese were argument from authority; argument from consequence; and argument by comparison (similes, examples, historical parallels, and analogies).[45] She adds that argument from authority involved quoting a text of some antiquity, reflecting the belief that the distilled wisdom of the past could be applied to the present. In the *Tso-chuan* Confucius says,

Names are used to generate credibility, credibility is used to protect the ritual vessels, ritual vessels are used to embody ritual actions, ritual actions are used to enact significance (*yi*), significance is used to produce benefit, and benefit is used to bring peace to the people. These are the important measures for effecting sociopolitical order. To loan them to others is to give them control of the sociopolitical order. And when sociopolitical order is lost, that the state will follow is an exorable fact.[46]

To use the name or perform the ritual action meaningfully entails drawing an analogy between past and present circumstances to evoke this vested significance.[47]

Edwin Black focuses on one particular aspect of criticism relevant to this study, the *exhortative discourse*. He states that two attributes of the style of exhortation bear upon the matter of clarity. One of these attributes is the extensive use of concrete description; the other is the frequent substitution of *is* or *will be* for *should* or *should be*. Furthermore, he says that since radical conversion, which is the end of exhortation, implies the acceptance of a belief as absolutely true, the exhorter commonly bases his appeal on what he claims to be realities. "Where the theoretician may conclude that there *ought* to be a revolution, or war, the exhorter, clad in the mantle of prophecy, proclaims that there *will* be."[48]

The next five researchers address differing elements of the "audience." These perspectives are necessary as a comparative basis for understanding the differences between a Vietnamese audience and a Western audience.

Black posits an intriguing essay addressing "character" in "The Second Persona." He asserts that most of us understand that the moral judgment of a text is a portentous act in the process of criticism, and that the terminal character of such a judgment works to close critical discussion rather than open or encourage it. He adds that the technical difficulty of making moral judgments of rhetorical discourses is that we are accustomed to thinking of discourses as objects, and we are not equipped to render moral judgments of objects—we do not appraise the discourse in itself except in a technical or prudential way.[49]

"Instead," Black writes, "I propose exploring the hypothesis that if students of communication could more proficiently explicate the saliently human dimensions of a discourse—if we could, in a sense, discover for a complex linguistic formulation a corresponding form of character—we should then be able to subsume that discourse under a moral order and thus satisfy our obligation to history."[50]

Black further states that the actual auditors look to the discourse they are attending for cues that tell them how they are to view the world, even beyond the expressed concerns, the overt propositional sense, of the discourse.

Each one of us, after all, defines himself by what he believes and does.... The quest for identity is the modern pilgrimage. And we look to one another for hints as to whom we should become. Perhaps these reflections do not apply to everyone, but they do apply to the persuasible, and that makes them germane to rhetoric.... The critic can see in the auditor implied by a discourse a model of what the rhetor would have his real auditor become. What the critic can find projected by the discourse is the image of a man, and though that man may never find actual embodiment, it is still a man that the image is of. This condition makes moral judgment possible, and it is at this point in the process of criticism that it can illuminatingly be rendered.[51]

Michael McGuire writes that Johann Gottlieb Fichte's "Addresses to the German Nation" participate in the contexts both of historical fact or political need and philosophical contemplation.[52] Given Fichte's conception that philosophy is both personal and practical, these contexts are not discrete: Fichte's philosophy is a social mission for him. McGuire adds that "there can be little doubt that in a non-nation suffering foreign rule, the potential if not the need for audience definition is great. Audiences in such circumstances may have a heightened susceptibility to nationalistic appeals. For Fichte, the task of positing an ego for his audience was both socially necessary and consistent with his philosophical activity."[53]

McGuire summarizes Fichte's attempts to reconstitute the German people, stating,

The explication of personae in the rhetorical discourses can significantly enhance our grasp of subjective reality—of the convictions people hold or want to hold about events. . . . In the definition of the German people Fichte was constrained by his rhetorical task and purpose—unity—from recourse to too much detail. Rather, he relied upon his posit of a kind of transcendent tribe to conform to the audience's susceptibilities or needs at the moment, and interlaced with his praises of their basic natural (and shared) virtue he depicts their ruinous past and present. In calling for a history of the Germans which will rouse their spirits, rather than merely record their deeds, Fichte reveals his Romantic tendency while at the same time portraying the poverty of many Germans' spirits. Outside of this subjectivism Fichte merely points at the Napoleonic occupation as a fact which, in its subjectivist meanings, shows up the past weaknesses and lights the way to the value of German unity.[54]

Another perspective is offered from Michael McGee's "In Search of 'The People': A Rhetorical Alternative."[55] He writes that most all of social theory has been warranted by understanding "humanity" to be a collective entity, "the people." And central to all of rhetorical theory has been a similar organic concept, the advocate's "audience." McGee contends that the consistent appearance in rhetorical literature of appeals to "the people," however, has been considered usual argumentative gymnastics. "Especially in analyzing *messages*, critics have taken 'people' and audience to be no more than plural abstractions of 'person' or 'individual,'" writes McGee, adding that, "in consequence, any appeal to a 'people' is almost by definition an argumentative fallacy and hence an 'irrational' form of persuasion."[56]

McGee concludes his article stating:
My argument here has been that through the analysis of rhetorical documents (particularly political myths), it should be possible to speak meaningfully, not of one's own,

but of *the people's* repertory of convictions, not as they ought to be, but as they *are* (or have been). When a writer works with rhetorical documents, he sees material forces, events, and themes in history *only as they have already been mediated or filtered by the Leader whose words he studies.* What he sees, in other words, is not a dialectical materialism, but rather a "rhetorical idealism." ... Pursuing a rhetorical alternative in defining "the people" leads one to the importance of recognizing the collective life as a condition of being the "audience" of those who pretend to lead the society.[57]

Maurice Charland writes about the effective power of constitutive rhetoric. He states that what is significant in constitutive rhetoric is that it positions the reader toward political, social, and economic action in the material world and it is in this positioning that its ideological character becomes significant. He states that for the purpose of analysis, this positioning of subjects as historical actors can be understood as a two-step process. First, audience members must be successfully interpellated; not all constitutive rhetorics succeed. Second, the tautological logic of constitutive rhetoric must necessitate action in the material world; constitutive rhetoric must require that its embodied subjects act freely in the social world to affirm their subject position. Charland concludes that "to be an embodied subject is to experience and act in a textualized world."[58]

Because ideology forms the ground for any rhetorical situation, a theory of ideological rhetoric must be mindful not only of arguments and ideographs, but of the very nature of the subjects that rhetoric both addresses and leads to come to be. Indeed, because the constitutive nature of rhetoric establishes the boundary of a subject's motives and experience, a truly ideological rhetoric must rework or transform subjects. A transformed ideology would require a transformed subject (not a dissolving of subjectivity). Such a transformation requires ideological and rhetorical work. This can proceed at two levels: (1) it can proceed at the level of the constitutive narrative itself, providing stories that through the identifactory principle shift and rework the subject and its motives; (2) it can also proceed at the aesthetic level of what Williams terms the "structure of feeling" and Grossberg describes as the "affective apparatus." Since, as Fisher observes, the truth of a narrative resides in its "fidelity," which is an aesthetic quality, new true narratives become possible as new modes of aesthetic experience emerge and gain social meaning. Ideological rhetorical practice is not restricted to explicitly political public address, but can include a range of aesthetic practices, including music, drama, architecture, and fashion, that elicit new modes of experience and being.[59]

John Hammerback argues in "Jose Antonio's Rhetoric of Fascism" that Antonio's rhetoric exemplifies how the fascist ideology invites and can be effectively embodied in the rhetor's substantive themes and arguments, second persona, and first or personal persona.[60] Hammerback suggests that when these rhetorical components are reciprocal and complementary, as in the case of Jose Antonio, they comprise a rhetorical formula that helps to explain his persuasion. He states that "[I]n their most potent form the rhetorical components seem to coalesce in a merger of the rhetor's thought and character which can reconstitute individuals into audiences capable of carrying out fascist policies."[61]

Hammerback insists that it is only by merging persona and ideas in discourse, by simultaneously identifying with and educating audiences through the agency of one's self as well as one's arguments, explanations, and themes, that this reconstitution can take place. He adds that in fascism's development in Spain, themes, arguments, personal persona, and second persona were not discrete categories of rhetorical appeal; they were reciprocally related parts of a synthesis that was essential to rhetorical and, hence, political success. The ideology of fascism invited particular rhetorical strategies that constrained the rhetor; and Jose Antonio closely conformed to the ideology's inherent directions for rhetorical success when he composed and communicated his message.[62]

In his effort to reconstitute audiences into agents to enact the fascist agenda, he (Antonio) combined his thought (themes and arguments) and his character (personae) into a message that flowed naturally from fascist ideology. Such a multi-level identification with audiences, according to Antczak, enables rhetors to reconstitute audiences. For those rhetorically redefined people, Jose Antonio and fascism fused to the point where the movement became a mere extension of the man.[63]

This historiography is best presented by reflecting on the interpretations of the biographers of Ho Chi Minh, the description of Vietnamese village politics, Vietnamese worldview assumptions, and Ho's rhetorical discourse to address the character of Ho Chi Minh and the concept of "reconstitutive rhetoric." The analysis involved extensive primary and secondary research, including examination of extants from university libraries, government, and private sources.

Information collected as primary sources concerning Ho Chi Minh is verified by Douglas Pike. Textual authenticity of secondary sources regarding Ho Chi Minh is verified through the process of what Tucker, Weaver, and Berryman-Fink call the *believability* criteria: (1) evaluation of the genuineness of the statement or document; (2) estimation of the credibility of the source; (3) discovery of other support independent of the source; and (4) appraisal of statements in light of the period under study.[64] The validity of the research findings was established by confirming consistency between the bibliographical accounts, historical and cultural analyses, and Ho's extant writings, which include *Selected Writings of Ho Chi Minh;* "Speech at the Tours Congress"; "Viet Nam Hon"; "Eight-Point Programme"; *Le Proces de la Colonisation Francaise;* "Monument to Dead Annamites"; "Some Considerations on the Colonial Question"; "Racial Hatred"; "Annamese Women and French Domination"; "An Open Letter to M. Albert Sarraut, Minister of Colonies"; "An Open Letter to M. Leon Archimbaud"; "An Appeal from the Peasant International to the Working Peasants in the Colonies"; "Annamese Peasant Conditions"; "Lenin and the Peoples of the East"; "Report on the National and Colonial Questions at the Fifth Congress of the Communist International"; "Indochina and the Pacific"; "Lynching"; *Thanh Nien;* "Lenin and the East"; *Duong Kach Menh* (Revolutionary Road); "French Colonization on Trial"; "Letter from Abroad"; and "An Appeal for General Insurrection." Extant poems include *Poems from a Prison Diary;* "After Prison, A

Walk in the Mountains"; "The Wife of the Deserter"; "The Child in Pin Yang Prison"; "Autumn Night"; "Hard Is the Road to Life"; and "Revolution."

The remaining biographies of Ho Chi Minh follow the same basic chronological format, that of: describing Vietnam's environment under colonial rule at the time of Ho's birth, early childhood and family, years of travel, beginnings as a revolutionary, years with the Comintern, Communism, the people's front, prison, and independence in 1945.

This next group of biographical materials were located in the Indochina Archives, Douglas Pike, Director, University of California–Berkeley. Accounting for source origination is incomplete for these biographies, many of which are newspaper articles. All are classified with a file (DRV), subject (BIOG), date, and sub-category (Ho Chi Minh) identification. They begin with: Author Unknown, "Official Ho Chi Minh Biography: Childhood (1890–1911)," no date; Renjo Maccinali, "Interview with Ho Chi Minh," *L'Unita* 15 March 1924; and Osip Mandel'stam, "Nguyen Ai Quoc—A Meeting with an International Communist," *Plamya* 36 (23 December 1923), Translator: Documentation Office, *Hoc Tap*. These sources have been used in the present study to explore the thought and character of Ho Chi Minh.

Extant Works of Ho Chi Minh

Ho Chi Minh's extant works used in this dissertation have been verified for their authenticity and accuracy in translation from Vietnamese into English.[65] There are two distinct developmental periods of Ho's rhetorical discourse: the first is his call for revolution and vision for a "new" and independent Vietnam, as witnessed through his writings, speeches, poems, et cetera between the period 1920–1940; the second is his initiation of the revolutionary movement beginning at Pac Bo in 1941 and culminating with his declaration of independence on 2 September 1945. The following are representative for those periods.

Period of Reconstitution: 1920–1940

Ho's "eight points of consideration" presented to the Versailles Peace Conference in 1920 sought freedom and equal rights for Vietnamese;[66] "Speech at the Tours Congress" debuted the issue of French imperialism and oppression in Indochina;[67] "Some Considerations on the Colonial Question" focuses on poverty in Indochina and other French colonies, the indifference of the ruling class of France toward the colonies, the ignorance of the natives, prejudices, and the fierceness of repression;[68] "Racial Hatred" cites specific examples of inhumane treatment of the Indochinese by French citizens in Indochina;[69] "Annamese Women and French Domination" details French sadism, cruelties, and violence performed on Vietnamese women by those symbolizing French gallantry;[70] "Annamese Peasant Conditions" is a condemnation of France's economic imperialism and taxation practices in Vietnam;[71] "Indochina and the Pacific" describes the failure of the French Ministry of Colonies plan for redeveloping the economic state of Indochina;[72] "The Failure of French Colonization" is a detailed account of resources taken from Indochina by the French without proper reimbursement;[73] "Appeal Made by Comrade Nguyen Ai Quoc on the Occasion of the Founding of the Party 3 February 1930" is both a call to revolution and an appeal for Party action.[74]

Period of Revolution: 1941–1945

This period begins with a "Letter from Abroad," which outlines the new Party name and objectives and calls for a general uprising throughout Indochina;[75] *Poems from a Prison Diary* are both a reflection of prison life and messages to Vietminh comrades;[76] and the "Instruction to Establish the Viet-Nam Propaganda Unit for National Liberation" establishes the first main force of the guerrilla unit the Viet-Nam People's Army, later to become the North Vietnamese Armed Forces.[77]

CHAPTER SUMMARY

The text includes six chapters. The first chapter introduces the study. The second chapter describes the research methodology and includes a review of existing literature.

The third chapter introduces Ho Chi Minh's biographical background. Events are highlighted that were integral in the development of his character and leadership, from his birth on 19 May 1890 up to and including the time when he declared Vietnam an independent nation 9 September 1945.

The fourth chapter compares worldview assumptions of classical Chinese philosophy to those of classical Western philosophy, and explores primary agents responsible for the traditional Vietnamese political system: Confucianism and the "Mandate of Heaven" (T'ien-ming). Historically, China was *the* dominant influence on Vietnamese sociopolitical, philosophical, and, in part, religious foundations that shaped Ho's contemporary Vietnam. The pattern of Vietnamese government prior to French colonialism modeled the pattern of imperial government in China, as it existed for more than two thousand years up to the establishment of the Chinese Republic in 1912, which also has been called "the Confucian state."[78] This chapter identifies the key elements of political life that Ho employed or used as rhetorical appeals during his struggle for Vietnam's independence.

The fifth chapter focuses on the Confucian concept of the "superior man," or the *Chun tzu*, the central idea of Confucianism that every human being cherishes the aspiration to become a superior man. Also, this chapter explores the "theory of imitation," or power by example, resulting in the doctrine "government by example."

The sixth chapter analyzes extant selections of Ho's rhetorical discourse: speeches, letters, poems, and newspaper articles. These are integrated with primary and secondary accounts of his character. The development of the Vietnamese persona is much more complex than that of the West; and a Vietnamese leader's "public" persona bears far more influence on an individual than his western counterpart. This chapter explains *how* Ho used his character as a *rhetorical device* in his efforts to reconstitute his audience.

Conclusions are detailed in the seventh chapter.

NOTES

1. Douglas Pike is considered by academicians and historians to be the foremost U.S. expert on the Vietnam War, and one of this country's leading translators of the language. Pike was an officer in the U.S. Foreign Service in Vietnam in the 1960s and has written many texts on the war. For many years he had been the curator of the Indochinese Archives at the University of California–Berkeley. He has since moved the archives to Texas Tech University.

2. Dr. Ho Ting Hui is professor of Chinese studies at the Department of Anthropology, Florida State University; and Dr. Jensen Chung is professor of communication at the Department of Communication, San Francisco State University.

3. Many authors writing about the Vietnamese revolution were journalists, who wrote from their own experiences.

4. McAlister writes that when Mus was a small child he went to Vietnam, where his father founded the colonial education system shortly before World War I. He stayed on to become a scholar of Vietnamese and Southeast Asian culture at the Ecole Francaise d'Extreme–Orient in Hanoi. See John T. McAlister Jr., *Vietnam: The Origins of Revolution* (New York: Alfred A. Knopf, 1969), vii.

5. Most of Mus' notes, papers, manuscripts, texts, et cetera were written in French, which McAlister translated with the help of Mus before his death, and subsequently, with the aid of French scholars familiar with Mus and his work. See John T. McAlister Jr. and Paul Mus, *The Vietnamese and Their Revolution* (New York: Harper and Row, 1969), xii.

6. Ibid.

7. John T. McAlister Jr. and Paul Mus, *The Vietnamese and Their Revolution.*

8. Douglas Pike, *History of Vietnamese Communism, 1925–1976* (Stanford, Calif.: Hoover Institution Press, 1978).

9. William J. Duiker, *The Rise of Nationalism in Vietnam, 1900–1941* (Ithaca, N.Y.: Cornell University Press, 1976).

10. William J. Duiker, *Vietnam: Nation in Revolution* (Boulder, Colo.: Westview, 1983).

11. Ellen Hammer, *Vietnam: Yesterday and Today* (New York: Holt, Rinehart and Winston, 1966), 134.

12. Stein Tonnesson, *The Vietnamese Revolution of 1945: Roosevelt, Ho Chi Minh, and de Gaulle in a World at War* (London: Sage, 1991).

13. Jacques Dalloz, *The War in Indochina, 1945–54* (Dublin: Gill and Macmillan, 1987).

14. Jean Chesneaux, *The Vietnamese Nation: Contribution to a History* (Sydney: Current Book Distributors, 1966).

15. John DeFrancis, *Colonialism and Language Policy in Vietnam* (The Hague: Mouton Publishers, 1977).

16. Hue-Tam Ho Tai, *Radicalism and the Origins of the Vietnamese Revolution* (Cambridge: Harvard University Press, 1992). Also, many authors who wrote about the war in Vietnam were journalists and not scholars.

17. David Marr, *Vietnamese Anticolonialism, 1885–1925* (Berkeley and Los Angeles: University of California Press, 1971).

18. David Marr, *Vietnamese Tradition on Trial, 1920–1945* (Berkeley and Los Angeles: University of California Press, 1981).

19. Ralph Smith, *Viet-Nam and the West* (Ithaca, N.Y.: Cornell University Press, 1968).

20. Wm. Theodore de Bary, ed., *Sources of Chinese Tradition* (New York: Columbia University Press, 1960).

21. David L. Hall and Roger T. Ames, *Thinking through Confucius* (Albany: State University of New York Press, 1987).

22. Roger T. Ames, *Sun-Tzu: The Art of Warfare* (New York: Ballantine Books, 1993).

23. Herrlee G. Creel, *The Origins of Statecraft in China*, vol. 1, *The Western Chou Empire* (Chicago: University of Chicago Press, 1970).

24. Herrlee G. Creel, *Chinese Thought from Confucius to Mao Tse-tung* (Chicago: University of Chicago Press, 1953).

25. Herrlee G. Creel, *Sinism: A Study of the Evolution of the Chinese World-View* (Chicago: Open Court, 1929).

26. Herrlee G. Creel, *Confucius: The Man and the Myth* (New York: John Day, 1949).

27. E.R. Hughes, *Chinese Philosophy in Classical Times* (New York: E.P. Dutton, 1944).

28. Miles Meander Dawson, *The Basic Teachings of Confucius* (New York: New Home Library, 1942).

29. Lin Yutang, *The Wisdom of Confucius* (New York: Modern Library, 1938).

30. Mary Garrett, "Pathos Reconsidered from the Perspective of Classical Chinese Rhetorical Theories," *Quarterly Journal of Speech* 79 (1993), 19–39.

31. Xing Lu and David A. Frank, "On the Study of Ancient Chinese Rhetoric/*Bian*," *Western Journal of Communication* 57 (Fall 1993), 445–463.

32. Archimedes Patti, *Why Viet Nam? Prelude to America's Albatross* (Berkeley and Los Angeles: University of California Press, 1980). Please see "Biography of Ho Chi Minh," manuscript page 27; also in Bibliography; also see page 67 of manuscript footnote 225

33. Raymond K. Tucker, Richard L. Weaver, and Cynthia Berryman-Fink, *Research in Speech Communication* (Englewood Cliffs, N.J.: Prentice-Hall, 1981), 66.

34. Ibid., 69.

35. Ibid.

36. Ibid.

37. Frederick J. Antczak, *Thought and Character: The Rhetoric of Democratic Education* (Ames: Iowa State University Press, 1985), 101.

38. Ibid., 101.

39. Ibid., 101.

40. Richard A. Cherwitz, ed., *Rhetoric and Philosophy* (Hillsdale, N.J.: Erlbaum, 1990), 4.

41. James W. Hikins, "Realism and Its Implications for Rhetorical Theory," in *Rhetoric and Philosophy*, ed. Richard A. Cherwitz (Hillsdale, N.J.: Erlbaum, 1990), 23–24.

42. Barry Brummett, "Relativism and Rhetoric," in *Rhetoric and Philosophy*, ed. Richard A. Cherwitz (Hillsdale, N.J.: Erlbaum, 1990), 82.

43. Joaquin Barcelo, "Universal Language and Rhetoric," *Philosophy and Rhetoric* 14, no. 3 (Summer 1981), 139.

44. Ibid., 139.

45. Mary Garrett, "Asian Challenge," reprinted in Sonja K. Foss, Karen A. Foss, and Robert Trapp, *Contemporary Perspectives on Rhetoric* (Prospect Heights, Ill.: Waveland, 1991), 299.

46. Hall and Ames, *Thinking through Confucius*, 273.

47. Ibid.

48. Edwin Black, *Rhetorical Criticism: A Study in Method* (Chicago: Macmillan, 1965), 143.

49. Edwin Black, "The Second Persona," *Quarterly Journal of Speech* 56, no. 2 (April 1970), 109–119.

50. Ibid., 110.

51. Ibid., 113.

52. Michael D. McGuire, "Rhetoric, Philosophy, and the Volk: Johann Gottlieb Fichte's *Addresses to the German Nation*," *Quarterly Journal of Speech* 62 (April 1976), 135–144.

53. Ibid., 139.

54. Ibid., 144.

55. Michael C. McGee, "In Search of 'The People': A Rhetorical Alternative," *Quarterly Journal of Speech* 61 (October 1975), 235–249.

56. Ibid., 236.

57. Ibid., 236.

58. Charland, "Constitutive Rhetoric," 133–150.

59. Ibid., 148.

60. John C. Hammerback, "Jose Antonio's Rhetoric of Fascism," *Southern Communication Journal* 59, no. 3 (Spring 1994), 181–195.

61. Ibid., 183.

62. Ibid., 184.

63. Ibid., 192.

64. Tucker, Weaver, and Berryman-Fink, *Research in Speech Communication*, 84.

65. Extants were located under the direction and approval of Douglas Pike, Director of the Indochina Archives, University of California–Berkeley.

66. Versailles Peace Conference.

67. The Tours Congress was the Eighteenth National Congress of the French Socialist Party held from 25–30 December 1920. In this congress, Nguyen Ai Quoc sided with the left wing and, together with other comrades, approved the resolution to found the French Communist Party and join the Third International.

68. Printed in *L'Humanite*, 25 May 1922.

69. Printed in *Le Paria*, 1 July 1922.

70. Printed in *Le Paria*, 1 August 1922.

71. Printed in *La Vie Ouvriere*, 4 January 1924.

72. Printed in *La Correspondance Internationale* 18 (1924).

73. Printed in *La Correspondence Internationale* 26 (1924).

74. This is a speech delivered by Ho Chi Minh representing the Communist Internationale. This document is considered one of the important documents necessary for the study of the Party's strategic and tactical lines.

75. The Eighth Plenum of the Central Committee of the Communist Party of Indochina, held at Pac Bo (Cao Bang Province) 10–19 May 1941, decided on a new line highlighting the slogan "national liberation," establishing the Viet Minh Front, changing the names of various mass organizations into Associations for National Salvation, and speed-

ing up the preparations for an abortive armed uprising against the French on 6 June 1941. This letter calls on revolutionary fighters at home, together with all other Vietnamese, to rise up and overthrow the Japanese and the French.

76. Ho Chi Minh, *Poems from a Prison Diary* (Hanoi: Foreign Languages Publishing House, 1959).

77. The Viet-Nam Propaganda Unit for National Liberation was set up on 22 December 1944, from small guerrilla units that had formerly operated in the provinces of Co Bang and Lang Son. At the beginning, it comprised thirty-four men and officers under the command of Vo Nguyen Giap, a history professor who in 1945 became the commanding general of the Viet-Nam People's Army, which grew out of that first guerrilla unit.

78. Creel, *The Origins of Statecraft in China*, 44.

Bibliography

BOOKS

Ames, R.T. (1993). *Sun-Tzu: The Art of Warfare*. New York: Ballantine Books.

Antczak, F.J. (1985). *Thought and Character: The Rhetoric of Democratic Education*. Ames: Iowa State University Press.

Archer, J. (1971). *Ho Chi Minh: Legend of Hanoi*. Folkestone, U.K.: Bailey Brothers and Swinfen.

Black, E. (1965). *Rhetorical Criticism: A Study in Method*. Chicago:.

Brummett, B. (1990). Relativism and Rhetoric. In *Rhetoric and Philosophy*, ed. Richard A. Cherwitz, 1–19. Hillsdale, N.J.: Erlbaum.

Bui, L. (1965). *Days With Ho Chi Minh*. Hanoi: Foreign Languages Publishing House.

Cherwitz, R.A. (ed.). (1990). *Rhetoric and Philosophy*. Hillsdale, N.J.: Erlbaum.

Chesneaux, J. (1966). *The Vietnamese Nation: Contribution to a History*. Sydney: Current Book Distributors.

Creel, H.G. (1929). *Sinism: A Study of the Evolution of the Chinese World-View*. Chicago: Open Court.

———. (1949). *Confucius: The Man and the Myth*. New York: John Day.

———. (1953). *Chinese Thought from Confucius to Mao Tse-tung*. Chicago: University of Chicago Press.

———. (1970). *The Origins of Statecraft in China*. Vol. 1, *The Western Chou Empire*. Chicago: University of Chicago Press.

Dalloz, J. (1987). *The War in Indochina, 1945–54*. Dublin: Gill and Macmillan.

Das, S.R.M. (1950). *Ho Chi Minh—Nationalist or Soviet Agent?* Bombay: R. Swarup.

Dawson, M.M. (1942). *The Basic Teachings of Confucius*. New York: New York Home Library.

de Bary, W.T. (ed.). (1960). *Sources of Chinese Tradition*. New York: Columbia University Press.

DeFrancis, J. (1977). *Colonialism and Language Policy in Vietnam*. The Hague: Mouton Publishers.

Duiker, W.J. (1976). *The Rise of Nationalism in Vietnam, 1900–1941*. Ithaca, N.Y.: Cornell University Press.

———. (1983). *Vietnam: Nation in Revolution.* Boulder, Colo.: Westview.

Fall, B. (1964). *The Two Vietnams.* New York: Frederick A. Praeger.

———. (1967). *Ho Chi Minh on Revolution: Selected Writings, 1920–66.* New York: Frederick A. Praeger.

———. (1967). *Last Reflections on a War.* Garden City, N.Y.: Doubleday.

Fenn, C. (1973). *Ho Chi Minh: A Biographical Introduction.* New York: Charles Scribner's Sons.

———, trans. (1960). *Oeuvres Choises.* Hanoi: Foreign Languages Publishing House.

Fisher, G. (1980). *International Negotiation: A Cross-Cultural Perspective.* Washington, D.C.: Library of Congress, Intercultural Press.

Foss, S.K., K.A. Foss, and R. Trapp, eds. (1991). *Contemporary Perspectives on Rhetoric.* Prospect Heights, Ill.: Waveland.

Fung, Y.-L., and D. Bodde, trans. (1937). *A History of Chinese Philosophy: The Period of the Philosophers.* Peiping: Henri Vetch. China.

Halberstam, D. (1971). *Ho.* New York: Random House.

Hall, D.L., and Ames, R.T. (1987). *Thinking through Confucius.* Albany: State University of New York Press.

Hammer, E. (1966). *Vietnam: Yesterday and Today.* New York: Holt, Rinehart and Winston.

Hickey, G.C. (1964). *Village in Vietnam.* New Haven, Conn.: Yale University Press.

Hikins, J.W. (1990). Realism and Its Implications for Rhetorical Theory. In *Rhetoric and Philosophy,* ed. Richard A. Cherwitz, 1–19. Hillsdale, N.J.: Erlbaum.

Hoang, V.C. (1964). *From Colonialism to Communism: A Case History of North Vietnam.* New York: Frederick A. Praeger.

Hodgkin, T. (1981). *Vietnam: The Revolutionary Path.* London: Macmillan.

Hue-Tam, H.T. (1992). *Radicalism and the Origins of the Vietnamese Revolution.* Cambridge: Harvard University Press.

Hughes, E.R. (1944). *Chinese Philosophy in Classical Times.* New York: Dutton.

Huyen, N.K. (1971). *Vision Accomplished? The Enigma of Ho Chi Minh.* New York: Macmillan.

Lacouture, J. (1968). *Ho Chi Minh: A Political Biography.* New York: Random House.

Luong, Hy.V. (1992). *Revolution in the Village: Tradition and Transformation in North Vietnam, 1925–1988.* Honolulu: University of Hawaii Press.

Marr, D. (1971). *Vietnamese Anticolonialism, 1885–1925.* Berkeley and Los Angeles: University of California Press.

(1981). *Vietnamese Tradition on Trial, 1920–1945.* Berkeley and Los Angeles: University of California Press.

McAlister, J.T. Jr. (1969). *Vietnam: The Origins of Revolution.* New York: Alfred A. Knopf.

McAlister, J.T. Jr. and P. Mus. (1970). *The Vietnamese and Their Revolution.* New York: Harper and Row.

Minh, H.C. (1959). *Poems from a Prison Diary.* Hanoi: Foreign Languages Publishing House.

———. (1966). *Prison Diary.* Trans. Aileen Palmer. Hanoi: Foreign Languages Publishing House.

The Selected Works of Ho Chi Minh.

Neumann-Hoditz, R. (1972). *Portrait of Ho Chi Minh: An Illustrated Biography.* Trans. J. Hargreaves. Hamburg: Herder and Herder.

Oliver, R. (1971). *Culture and Communication in Ancient India and China.* Syracuse, N.Y.: Syracuse University Press.

Patti, A. (1980). *Why Vietnam? Prelude to America's Albatross.* Berkeley and Los Angeles: University of California Press.

Pham, K.V. (1990). *The Vietnamese Culture: An Introduction.* San Diego, Calif.: Pham Kim Vinh Research Institute.

Pike, D. (1966). *Viet Cong.* Cambridge: MIT Press.

(1978). *History of Vietnamese Communism, 1925–1976.* Stanford, Calif.: Hoover Institution Press.

Ray, S. (1966). *Vietnam Seen from East and West.* New York: Frederick A. Praeger.

Reischauer, E.O., and J.K. Fairbank. (1958). *East Asia: The Great Tradition.* Boston: Houghton Mifflin.

Sainteny, J. (1972). *Ho Chi Minh and His Vietnam: A Personal Memoir.* Chicago: Cowles Book Company.

SarDesai, D.R. (1992). *Vietnam: The Struggle for National Unity.* San Francisco: Westview.

Shaplen, R. (1965). *The Lost Revolution.* New York: Harper and Row.

Smith, R. (1968). *Viet-Nam and the West.* Ithaca, N.Y.: Cornell University Press.

Tonnesson, S. (1991). *The Vietnamese Revolution of 1945: Roosevelt, Ho Chi Minh, and de Gaulle in a World at War.* London: Sage.

Truong, C. (1966). *President Ho Chi Minh: Beloved Leader of the Vietnamese People.* Hanoi: Foreign Languages Publishing House.

Tu, W.M. (1976). *Centrality and Commonality: An Essay on Chung-Yung.* Honolulu: University of Hawaii Press.

Tucker, R.K., R.L. Weaver, and C. Berryman-Fink. (1981). *Research in Speech Communication.* Englewood Cliffs, N.J.: Prentice-Hall.

Warby, W. (1972). *Ho Chi Minh and the Struggle for an Independent Vietnam.* London: Merlin.

Watson, B., trans. (1964). *Han Fei Tzu: Basic Writings.* New York: Columbia University Press.

Woodside, A.B. (1976). *Community and Revolution in Modern Vietnam.* Boston: Houghton Mifflin.

Yutang, L. (1938). *The Wisdom of Confucius.* New York: Modern Library.

JOURNALS

Barcelo, J. (1981). Universal Language and Rhetoric. *Philosophy and Rhetoric* 14, no. 3, pp. 139–151.

Black, E. (1970). The Second Persona. *Quarterly Journal of Speech* 2, pp. 109–119.

Charland, M. (1987). Constitutive Rhetoric: The Case of the Peuple Quebecois. *Quarterly Journal of Speech* 2, pp. 133–150.

Crump, J., and Dreher, J. (March 1951). Peripatetic Rhetors of the Warring Kingdoms. *Central States Speech Journal* 2, pp. 15–17.

————.(March 1952). Pre-Han Persuasion: The Legalist School. *Central States Speech Journal* 3, pp. 10–14.

Garrett, M. (1993). *Pathos* Reconsidered from the Perspective of Classical Chinese Rhetorical Theories. *Quarterly Journal of Speech* 79, pp. 19–39.

Hammerback, J.C. (1994). Jose Antonio's Rhetoric of Fascism. *Southern Journal of Communication* 3, pp. 181–195.

Hammerback, J.C., and R.J. Jensen. (1994). Ethnic Heritage as Rhetorical Legacy: The Plan of Delano. *Quarterly Journal of Speech* 80, no. 1, p. 67.

Lu, X., and D.A. Frank. (1993). On the Study of Ancient Chinese Rhetoric/*Bian*. *Quarterly Journal of Speech* 57, pp. 445–463.

McGee, M. (1975). In Search of "The People": A Rhetorical Alternative. *Quarterly Journal of Speech* 3, pp. 235–249.

McGuire, M.D. (April 1976). Rhetoric, Philosophy , and the Volk: Johann Gottlieb Fichte's Addresses to the German Nation. *Quarterly Journal of Speech* 62, pp. 135–144.

Mus, P. (September 1949). The Role of the Village in Vietnamese Politics. *Public Affairs* 22, pp. 266–280.

Oliver, R.T. (1969). The Rhetorical Tradition in China: Confucius and Mencius. *Today's Speech* 17, pp. 3–8.

Reynolds, B. (1969). Lao Tzu: Persuasion through Inaction and Non-Speaking. *Today's Speech* 17, pp. 23–25.

Tran, V.D. (1976). The Rhetoric of Revolt: Ho Chi Minh as Communicator. *Journal of Communication* 26, no. 4, pp. 142–147.

NEWSPAPERS

Minh, H.C. (1922). Some Considerations on the Colonial Question. *L' Humanite*.

(1924). Annamese Peasant Conditions. *La Vie Ouvriere* .

(1924). The Failure of French Colonization. *La Correspondence Internationale* 26.

———. (1924). Indochina and the Pacific. *La Correspondence Internationale* 18.

Summary Biography of President Ho Chi Minh. (September 8, 1969). *Vietnam Courier*.

INSTITUTIONS

United States. University of California–Berkeley. Indochina Archives File DRV, Subj BIOG, Date July 1939, Sub-cat. Ho Chi Minh. "The Line of the Party during the Period of the Democratic Front (1936–1939)," *Tuyen Tap*, July 1939. Reprinted by Su That Publishing House, Hanoi, 1960, pp. 196.

United States. University of California–Berkeley. Indochina Archives. File DRV. Subj BIOG. Sub-cat Ho Chi Minh. Date December 1920. "Speech at the Tours Congress."

United States. University of California–Berkeley. Indochina Archives. File DRV. Subj BIOG. Date 1922. Sub-cat Ho Chi Minh; *Le Paria*. "Annamese Women and French Domination."

United States. University of California–Berkeley. Indochina Archives. File DRV. Subj BIOG. Date February 1930. Sub-cat Ho Chi Minh. "Appeal Made by Comrade Nguyen Ai Quoc on the Occasion of the Founding of the Party 3 February 1930."

United States. University of California–Berkeley. Indochina Archives. File DRV. Subj BIOG. Date August 1953. Sub-cat Ho Chi Minh. *Ho Chi Minh and the Communist Movement in IndoChina: A Study in the Exploitation of Nationalism*.

United States. University of California–Berkeley. Indochina Archives. File DRV. Subj BIOG. Date 23 December 1923. Sub-cat Ho Chi Minh. *Plamya*. Mandel'stam, O. *Hoc Tap*.

United States. University of California–Berkeley. Indochina Archives. File DRV. Subj BIOG. Date June 1970. Sub-cat Ho Chi Minh. *Selected Writings, 1920–1969*.

Index

About the Author

PETER A. DECARO teaches in the Department of Communication Studies at California State University, Stanislaus.